COLLINS

CHEERFUL COOKING

EUROPEAN FAVOURITES

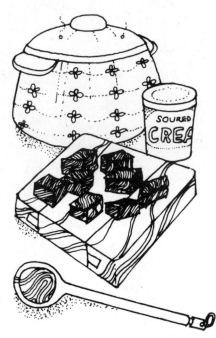

© Wm. Collins Sons & Co. Ltd. 1973
First published 1973
This edition 1978
ISBN 0 00 435274 2

Devised, edited and designed by Youé and Spooner Ltd.

Printed in Great Britain by Collins Clear-Type Press

COLLINS CHEERFUL COOKING

EUROPEAN FAVOURITES

CAROL WRIGHT

COLLINS
LONDON & GLASGOW

Useful weights and measures

WEIGHT EQUIVALENTS

Avoirdupois		Metric
1 ounce	=	28·35 grammes
1 pound	=	453·6 grammes
2·3 pounds	=	1 kilogram

LIQUID MEASUREMENTS

$\frac{1}{4}$ pint	=	$1\frac{1}{2}$ decilitres
$\frac{1}{2}$ pint	=	$\frac{1}{4}$ litre
scant 1 pint	=	$\frac{1}{2}$ litre
$1\frac{3}{4}$ pints	=	1 litre
1 gallon	=	4·5 litres

HANDY LIQUID MEASURES

1 pint	=	20 fluid ounces	=	32 tablespoons
$\frac{1}{2}$ pint	=	10 fluid ounces	=	16 tablespoons
$\frac{1}{4}$ pint	=	5 fluid ounces	=	8 tablespoons
$\frac{1}{8}$ pint	=	$2\frac{1}{2}$ fluid ounces	=	4 tablespoons
$\frac{1}{16}$ pint	=	$1\frac{1}{4}$ fluid ounces	=	2 tablespoons

HANDY SOLID MEASURES

				Approximate
Almonds, ground	1 oz.	=	$3\frac{3}{4}$ level tablespoons
Arrowroot	1 oz.	=	4 level tablespoons
Breadcrumbs fresh	1 oz.	=	7 level tablespoons
dried	1 oz.	=	$3\frac{1}{4}$ level tablespoons
Butter and Lard	1 oz.	=	2 level tablespoons
Cheese, grated	1 oz.	=	$3\frac{1}{2}$ level tablespoons
Chocolate, grated	1 oz.	=	3 level tablespoons
Cocoa	1 oz.	=	$2\frac{3}{4}$ level tablespoons
Desiccated Coconut	1 oz.	=	$4\frac{1}{2}$ tablespoons
Coffee — Instant	1 oz.	=	4 level tablespoons
Ground	1 oz.	=	4 tablespoons
Cornflour	1 oz.	=	$2\frac{1}{2}$ tablespoons
Custard powder	1 oz.	=	$2\frac{1}{2}$ tablespoons
Curry Powder and Spices	1 oz.	=	5 tablespoons
Flour	1 oz.	=	2 level tablespoons
Gelatine, powdered	1 oz.	=	$2\frac{1}{2}$ tablespoons
Rice, uncooked	1 oz.	=	$1\frac{1}{2}$ tablespoons
Sugar, caster and granulated	1 oz.	=	2 tablespoons
Icing sugar	1 oz.	=	$2\frac{1}{2}$ tablespoons
Syrup	1 oz.	=	1 tablespoon
Yeast, granulated	1 oz.	=	1 level tablespoon

AMERICAN MEASURES

16	fluid ounces	=	1 American pint
8	fluid ounces	=	1 American standard cup
0·50	fluid ounces	=	1 American tablespoon *(slightly smaller than British Standards Institute tablespoon)*
0·16	fluid ounces	=	1 American teaspoon

AUSTRALIAN MEASURES
(Cup, Spoon and Liquid Measures)

These are the measures in everyday use in the Australian family kitchen. The spoon measures listed below are from the ordinary household cutlery set.

CUP MEASURES

(Using the 8-liquid-ounce cup measure)

1 cup flour	4 oz.
1 cup sugar *(crystal or caster)*	8 oz.
1 cup icing sugar *(free from lumps)*	5 oz.
1 cup shortening *(butter, margarine, etc.)*	8 oz.
1 cup honey, golden syrup, treacle	10 oz.
1 cup brown sugar *(lightly packed)*	4 oz.
1 cup brown sugar *(tightly packed)*	5 oz.
1 cup soft breadcrumbs	2 oz.
1 cup dry breadcrumbs *(made from fresh breadcrumbs)*	3 oz.
1 cup packet dry breadcrumbs	4 oz.
1 cup rice *(uncooked)*	6 oz.
1 cup rice *(cooked)*	5 oz.
1 cup mixed fruit or individual fruit such as sultanas, etc.	4 oz.
1 cup grated cheese	4 oz.
1 cup nuts *(chopped)*	4 oz.
1 cup coconut	$2\frac{1}{2}$ oz.

SPOON MEASURES

	Level Tablespoon
1 oz. flour	2
1 oz. sugar *(crystal or caster)*	$1\frac{1}{2}$
1 oz. icing sugar *(free from lumps)*	2
1 oz. shortening	1
1 oz. honey	1
1 oz. gelatine	2
1 oz. cocoa	3
1 oz. cornflour	$2\frac{1}{2}$
1 oz. custard powder	$2\frac{1}{2}$

LIQUID MEASURES

(Using 8-liquid-ounce cup)

1 cup liquid	8 oz
$2\frac{1}{2}$ cups liquid	20 oz. (1 pint)
2 tablespoons liquid	1 oz.
1 gill liquid	5 oz. ($\frac{1}{4}$ pint)

Metric equivalents and oven temperatures are not listed here as they are included in all the recipes throughout the book.

When using the metric measures, in some cases it may be necessary to cut down the amount of liquid used. This is in order to achieve a balanced recipe and the correct consistency, as 1oz equals, in fact, 28·35gm.

Introduction

The great increase in holidays abroad in the past 20 years has had a striking influence on our eating habits. We have tried foreign foods on holiday, liked them and wanted to cook them at home. In fact we have become much more adventurous. In the old days the British traveller regarded foreign food with suspicion. Now fettucini and fondue, pizza and paella are accepted, as everyday dishes or party fare.

Not only has the traveller found exciting dishes to serve, but new ideas also come to him as foreign restaurants of all kinds open up in almost every city.

Along with this it has become much easier to get the correct ingredients to make those dishes from abroad at home. Most big supermarkets sell a wide selection of spices, herbs and other ingredients, and better grocers stock a variety of Continental foods. Even convenience foods are getting a Continental touch. One chain store sells ready-to-cook lasagne and Quiche Lorraine, cheesecakes and cannelloni. And a soup firm once told me that they watched which countries people visited for their holidays and then produced their next season's range based on recipes from those countries.

I spend four or five months of each year travelling around, and love trying out the foods of each country. It is one way of learning a lot about different people. 'Tell me what you eat and I will tell you what sort of a man you are,' said one philosopher. There are many fascinating recipes which you can learn from other countries to enrich your own traditions. Many of the recipes that follow are classics which have been adapted to English ways of cooking: others are those I've relished on my travels and hope you will enjoy.

Hors d'oeuvre

This chapter contains plenty of new ideas for meal starters. Some of the recipes, such as avocado dip, also make good cocktail fare and go well with pre-dinner drinks.

We use a French word for the items that start a meal. Certainly Continental people have some delightful ideas for small appetizers that can be handed round with pre-lunch or dinner drinks or served at the table. The Spanish have their *tapas* in the south, little savoury items speared on cocktail sticks offered free in the bars, each bar competing to have the best.

In northern Europe, in Scandinavia, there is the cold table tradition – a vast spread of cold dishes, with some hot, served usually at lunchtime. Among the cold dishes there are many recipes, such as herring salads, that make ideal hors d'oeuvre.

The Dutch too have casual, almost snack, lunchtime meals and many of the little appetizers they offer like cheese croquettes are delightful to serve on their own. The French and Belgians have various ways of serving eggs and in the hotter climates of the south the Greeks, Southern French and Spanish have attractive ways of presenting vegetables as meal starters.

AVOCADO DIP
Serves 4

A dip to go with the French idea of *crudités* – raw pieces of vegetable served as an appetizer.

2 large ripe avocados
juice of 1 lemon
2 small sticks celery, finely chopped
1 small green pepper, de-seeded and very finely chopped
1 teaspoon dry mustard
salt and black pepper
oil to blend

1. Skin the avocado, remove the stone and mash the flesh.
2. Add the lemon juice, celery, green pepper and mustard and mix well. Season to taste with salt and black pepper. Blend to a soft consistency with oil.
3. Serve with a selection of small pieces of raw vegetables – celery, carrot, cauliflower florets, radishes etc.

DANISH BLUE MOUSSE
Serves 6–8

4oz (100gm) Danish blue cheese
4oz (100gm) Samsoe cheese
½ pint (250ml) double cream
1oz (25gm) almonds, chopped and toasted
2 tablespoons water
½oz (12gm) gelatine
2 egg whites
salt and pepper
mustard
maraschino cherries and lettuce hearts to garnish

1. Finely grate both cheeses into a large bowl.
2. Partially whip cream and add with almonds to cheeses.
3. Add the water to gelatine in a small bowl and place over a pan of hot water until the gelatine is dissolved. Allow to cool.
4. Whip the egg whites stiffly and fold into the cheese mixture; season with salt, pepper and mustard.
5. Fold in the gelatine.
6. Pour mixture into a 1-lb (½-kilo) loaf tin and put in a cool place to set.
7. When required, turn the mousse out and garnish with maraschino cherries and lettuce hearts. Serve with melba toast and butter.

CAMEMBERT MOUSSE
Serves 4

A light cheese dish from France to serve either before or after dinner.

6 portions Camembert cheese
1oz (25gm) butter, melted
2 portions Petit Suisse cheese
6 tablespoons double cream
2 level teaspoons made mustard
2 teaspoons finely chopped parsley
watercress to garnish

1. Discard the outer rinds from the Camembert.
2. Pound the cheese until smooth together with the melted butter.
3. Add Petit Suisse and beat well.
4. Lightly whip the cream and add to the cheese mixture.
5. Stir in the mustard and parsley.
6. Shape into a mould and chill.
7. Serve garnished with watercress.

STUFFED EGGS
Serves 3–4

A popular hors d'oeuvre in France.

6 hard-boiled eggs
1 can sardines
1 teaspoon French mustard
1 teaspoon grated onion
2 teaspoons lemon juice
salt and pepper

1. Halve each egg and remove the yolk.
2. Cut a small slice off the rounded side of each half so that they will remain upright.
3. Push the yolks through a sieve and mash them thoroughly.
4. Mash the sardines with the remaining ingredients and then add the yolks. Blend well together.
5. Fill the whites with the mixture.
6. Serve the eggs on a large platter with radishes, spring onions and slices of lemon.

TARAMASALATA
Serves 4–6

A delicious fish pâté from Greece.

3oz (75gm) tarama (bottled carp roe)
1 small onion, finely grated
½ pint (250ml) olive oil
4–5 slices white bread, crusts removed
juice of 2–3 lemons

1. Mash tarama and add grated onion.
2. Add a little of the olive oil and beat thoroughly to a smooth paste.
3. Moisten bread with water and squeeze out excess liquid.
4. Continue beating tarama mixture, adding, alternately, small pieces of moistened bread, olive oil and lemon juice. Taramasalata should be beaten until cream-coloured.
5. Serve with crackers or spread on toast.

MARINATED HERRINGS
Serves 4

Salt herrings are very popular in Scandinavian countries and are served as hors d'oeuvre and salads.

2 salt herring fillets
½ pint (250ml) white wine vinegar
2oz (50gm) caster sugar
1¼ tablespoons chopped onion
6 black peppercorns, crushed
6 whole allspice, crushed
raw onion rings steeped in lemon juice and chopped chives to garnish

1. Rinse herring fillets and drain.
2. Cut crosswise into ¼-inch slices.
3. Mix together the vinegar, sugar, chopped onion, peppercorns and allspice and leave to stand for 10 minutes.
4. Pour the dressing over the herrings.
5. Garnish with onion rings and chives.
6. Leave in the refrigerator for 2–3 hours, or overnight.

DANISH HERRINGS
Serves 6

6 herrings, cleaned and boned
1 onion, sliced
6 cloves
1 teaspoon peppercorns
1 teaspoon salt
1 teaspoon sugar
1 bayleaf
⅓ pint (170ml) vinegar
scant ¼ pint (125ml) French dressing (see Basic recipes, page 100)
¼ pint (125ml) soured cream
4 tablespoons salad cream
onion salt
chopped chives or spring onions to garnish

1. Preheat oven to cool, 300 deg F or gas 2 (150 deg C).
2. Roll the herrings, skin side outside, from the head end to the tail – secure with wooden cocktail sticks.
3. Place in a casserole, add the sliced onion, seasonings, vinegar and French dressing.
4. Cover and bake in the centre of the oven for 2 hours. Leave in the dish to become cold.
5. Blend the soured cream and salad cream together; season with onion salt.
6. Serve the herrings on a dish with a little of the cooking liquor spooned over.
7. Garnish with chopped chives or spring onions and serve the soured cream sauce separately.

COUNTRY HERRING TERRINE
(Illustrated on page 17)
Serves 6

A French way of using herrings.

4 herrings, boned
salt and pepper
2 hard-boiled eggs
1 cooking apple, peeled and
coarsely grated
2oz (50gm) ground almonds
1 level teaspoon sugar
few lettuce leaves and
cucumber slices to garnish

1. Preheat oven to moderate,
350 deg F or gas 4 (180 deg C).
2. Lightly grill herring fillets.
3. Peel off skin and pound flesh
with a wooden spoon until
smooth.
4. Season well with salt and
pepper.
5. Slice eggs and arrange six
good slices in the bottom of a
greased 1½-pint (approximately
¾-litre) ovenproof pie dish or
terrine.
5. Chop the remaining egg finely
and mix together with apple,
ground almonds, sugar and
pounded herring. Smooth into the
ovenproof dish.
7. Cover with kitchen foil or lid
and stand dish in a roasting tin of
hot water.
8. Bake in the centre of the oven
for 40 minutes.
9. Remove from the oven and
leave to cool. Turn out of dish.
10. Garnish with lettuce leaves
and cucumber slices and serve
with fingers of toast, and butter.

HERRING KAASSLA
Serves 6

6oz (150gm) Gouda cheese
1 apple
6 sticks celery
6 gherkins
6oz (150gm) cooked peas
1 small packet mixed frozen
vegetables, cooked
salt and pepper
mayonnaise
6 rollmop herrings
6oz (150gm) grapes and
chopped parsley to garnish

1. Cut the cheese, apple, celery
and gherkins into small cubes.
2. Mix with peas, mixed
vegetables and seasoning.
3. Blend with a little mayonnaise
and pile on a serving dish.
4. Arrange rollmops over the top
and garnish with halved, pipped
grapes and chopped parsley.

CASTILLIAN COCKTAIL
Serves 4

4 tablespoons oil
1 tablespoon vinegar
2 tablespoons evaporated milk
salt and pepper
1 level teaspoon made mustard
1 level teaspoon lemon juice
1 teaspoon Worcestershire
sauce
4oz (100gm) button mushrooms
1oz (25gm) butter
4 tablespoons cubed melon
few lettuce leaves, shredded

1. Make a dressing by mixing the
oil, vinegar, evaporated milk,
seasoning, mustard, lemon juice
and Worcestershire sauce
together.
2. Slice the mushrooms thinly
and cook in a little butter. Drain
and leave to cool.
3. Toss the cubed melon,
mushrooms and lettuce with the
dressing.
4. Spoon into glasses and serve
chilled.

MUSHROOMS WITH CREAM
(Illustrated on page 17)
Serves 4

Cooked mushrooms are a popular
hors d'oeuvre in many
European countries.

1lb (½ kilo) mushrooms
2oz (50gm) butter
salt and pepper
parsley
¼–½ teaspoon tarragon
chives
1 lemon
1 teaspoon tomato purée
dash Worcestershire sauce
¼ pint (125ml) cream

1. Slice or quarter the
mushrooms.
2. Heat the butter in a
good-sized pan, add mushrooms
and season with salt and pepper.
3. Put a few sprigs of parsley,
tarragon, a few chopped chives, a
slither of lemon peel into a muslin
bag and add to the pan.
4. Cover the pan and simmer
until the mushrooms are tender.
5. Remove the muslin bag; blend
together the tomato purée,
Worcestershire sauce and cream
and pour over the mushrooms.
6. Keep on a low heat until the
sauce is well heated (do not allow
to boil) then turn into a hot
serving dish and serve with lemon
wedges.

MINIATURE HUNGARIAN CABBAGE ROLLS
Serves 4–6

1 large head cabbage
1 egg
8oz (200gm) minced beef
4oz (100gm) pork sausagemeat
3oz (75gm) onion, finely chopped
2¼oz (56gm) boiled long-grain rice (raw weight)
4 tablespoons milk
¾ teaspoon seasoned salt
¼ teaspoon seasoned pepper
1 packet goulash seasoning mix
1 can (1lb or ½ kilo) tomatoes
1 can (8oz or 200gm) tomato sauce

1. Preheat oven to moderate, 350 deg F or gas 4 (180 deg C).
2. Separate cabbage leaves and immerse them for 1 minute in boiling water until softened. Drain and remove centre stalks.
3. Beat the egg.
4. Add minced beef, pork sausagemeat, onion, rice, milk, seasoned salt, seasoned pepper and 1 tablespoon goulash seasoning mix.
5. Mix thoroughly with a fork.
6. Blend remaining goulash seasoning mix, tomatoes and tomato sauce in a saucepan.
7. Bring to a boil, reduce heat and simmer 15–20 minutes.
8. Cut softened cabbage leaves into 4-inch pieces.
9. Place about ½ tablespoon meat mixture on each cabbage leaf. Roll up securely. Place in large buttered shallow baking dish.
10. Pour tomato mixture over cabbage rolls, cover and bake in centre of the oven for 25–30 minutes.

RATATOUILLE 1
Serves 4

Ratatouille is a French recipe using aubergines and courgettes to make a hot or cold mixture which can be served as an hors d'oeuvre, or with a main course dish.

2 medium onions
1lb (½ kilo) tomatoes
3 small aubergines
salt
2 small green or red peppers
4 small courgettes
2 garlic cloves, peeled and crushed
3 tablespoons olive oil
¼ teaspoon Tabasco sauce
12 coriander seeds

1. Chop the onions and skin the tomatoes.
2. Cut the aubergines into ¼-inch cubes place in a colander and sprinkle with salt
3. Seed and cut the peppers into dice.
4. Slice the courgettes into ¼-inch slices.
5. Gently cook the chopped onion and crushed garlic in the oil.
6. Rinse the aubergines and dry on kitchen paper.
7. Add to the onion with courgettes, tomatoes and peppers.
8. Season with salt and Tabasco sauce.
9. Add the coriander seeds, cover closely and simmer very slowly for 40 minutes.

RATATOUILLE 2
Serves 4

Another way of making this French dish using canned soup.

4 tablespoons olive oil
8oz (200gm) aubergines, sliced
8oz (200gm) courgettes, sliced
2 medium onions, sliced
1 garlic clove, crushed
1 green pepper, de-seeded and sliced
8oz (200gm) mushrooms, washed and sliced
1 can (15oz or 375gm) cream of tomato soup
1 level teaspoon oregano

1. Preheat oven to moderate to moderately hot, 375 deg F or gas 5 (190 deg C).
2. Heat the oil in a large saucepan.
3. Fry the aubergines, courgettes, onions, garlic and pepper until the onion is translucent and the aubergine soft.
4. Transfer to a casserole and add the remaining ingredients.
5. Cover and cook in the centre of the oven for 2½ hours.

MUSHROOM AND BACON KROMESKIES
Serves 4

Small individual pies, or a large one, sliced, served hot or cold are good appetizers.

6oz (150gm) mushrooms
2oz (50gm) streaky bacon, de-rinded
1oz (25gm) butter
1 teaspoon grated onion
4oz (100gm) cottage cheese
salt and pepper
shortcrust pastry made with 8oz (200gm) flour (see Basic recipes, page 100)
fat for deep frying

1. Finely chop the mushrooms and bacon.
2. Toss in hot butter for about 1 minute. Stir in the onion and mix with the cottage cheese.
3. Season carefully with salt and pepper.
4. Roll out the pastry thinly and cut into 4-inch squares.
5. Put a spoonful of the mixture on each square, damp the edges of the pastry and fold over into a triangle. Press the edges together very firmly.
6. Fry in hot deep fat until golden and well risen.
7. Drain on kitchen paper. Serve with a green salad.

MALTESE CHEESE PIE
Serves 4–6

3 eggs
8oz (200gm) cottage cheese
2oz (50gm) cooked peas
1oz (25gm) parsley, chopped
¼ teaspoon salt
white pepper to taste
½ teaspoon mixed dried herbs or oregano
puff pastry using 8oz (200gm) flour (see Basic recipes, page 100)
beaten egg to glaze

1. Preheat oven to hot, 425 deg F or gas 7 (220 deg C).
2. Whisk eggs in a basin large enough to take all filling ingredients.
3. Press cheese through a sieve into the basin and mix well. Stir in peas, parsley, salt, pepper and herbs.
4. Roll out half the pastry to line a 6-inch (15-cm) flan ring. Pour in filling, brush edges with beaten egg and cover with remaining pastry.
5. Trim and pinch edges together; make a hole to allow steam to escape, and decorate with pastry leaves made from the trimmings.
6. Brush with beaten egg.
7. Place on the second shelf from the top of the oven for 15–20 minutes; reduce the heat to moderate, 350 deg F or gas 4 (180 deg C) when the top is risen and golden, move pie to a lower shelf and cook for a further 30 minutes.
8. Serve hot or cold.

FUNEN PIE
Serves 4–6

A cheese flan dish from Denmark.

shortcrust pastry made with 8oz (200gm) flour (see Basic recipes, page 100)
3oz (75gm) butter
8oz (200gm) onions, sliced
salt and pepper
1½oz (37gm) flour
½ pint (250ml) milk
pinch of dry mustard
4oz (100gm) Danish blue cheese
watercress to garnish

1. Preheat oven to hot, 425 deg F or gas 7 (220 deg C).
2. Roll out the pastry to line an 8-inch (20-cm) flan case. Roll out the trimmings into ½-inch strips and keep for decoration.
3. Melt 2oz (50gm) butter in a pan and add the onions.
4. Cover and cook until tender but not brown. Add salt and pepper.
5. Melt remaining butter.
6. Add the flour and gradually add the milk, stirring, to make a white sauce.
7. Mix in a little mustard, the cooked onions and the crumbled or grated cheese. Pour into the prepared pastry case.
8. Arrange the pastry strips in a lattice on top and bake in the centre of the oven for 15 minutes.
9. Reduce heat to moderate, 350 deg F or gas 4 (180 deg C) and cook for a further 15–20 minutes, until the pastry is brown.
10. Serve hot or cold.

QUICHE LORRAINE
Serves 4–6

A French flan, ideal to take on picnics or to serve with pre-dinner drinks.

shortcrust pastry made with 6oz (150gm) flour (see Basic recipes, page 100)
4oz (100gm) streaky bacon, de-rinded
3oz (75gm) Cheddar cheese, grated
2 eggs plus 1 egg yolk
½ pint (250ml) single cream or half milk and half single cream
1 teaspoon French mustard

1. Preheat oven moderate to moderately hot, 400 deg F or gas 6 (200 deg C).
2. Line an 8-inch (20-cm) flan ring with the pastry.
3. Cut the bacon rashers into small squares and cook them in a dry frying pan for a minute – until the fat runs out.
4. Put the grated cheese at the bottom of the flan and place the becon pieces on top.
5. Beat the eggs together with the extra yolk, the cream (or cream and milk) and the mustard.
6. Pour on to the bacon.
7. Bake for 30 minutes in the centre of the oven.

ALL-IN-ONE QUICHE LORRAINE
Serves 4–6

4oz (100gm) soft margarine
1 tablespoon water
6oz (150gm) plain flour
2 eggs
1 level teaspoon chopped
chives (optional)
¼ pint (125ml) single cream
½ level teaspoon salt
pinch of cayenne pepper
4oz (100gm) streaky bacon,
de-rinded, grilled and chopped

1. Preheat oven to moderate to
moderately hot, 400 deg F or gas 6
(200 deg C).
2. To make the pastry place the
margarine, water and 2
tablespoons of the flour in a
mixing bowl.
3. Cream with a fork for about
half a minute, until well mixed.
4. Stir in the remaining flour to
form a firm dough.
5. Roll out fairly thinly and line a
7-inch (18-cm) flan ring.
6. For the filling place all the
ingredients, except the bacon, in
a mixing bowl and whisk together
until well mixed.
7. Place the bacon in the bottom
of the flan and pour over the
mixture.
8. Bake in the centre of the oven
for 30–35 minutes, until filling has
set and pastry is cooked.

INDIVIDUAL SALAMI AND COTTAGE CHEESE QUICHES
(Illustrated on page 17)
Serves 4

An Italian influence on the
French recipe.

shortcrust pastry made with
5oz (125gm) flour (see Basic
recipes, page 100)
2oz (50gm) salami, finely sliced
and skinned, plus 4 slices to
garnish
1 small onion, grated
¼ level teaspoon mixed dried
herbs
8oz (200gm) cottage cheese
2 eggs, beaten
salt and pepper
few lettuce leaves and black
olives to garnish

1. Preheat oven to moderate to
moderately hot, 400 deg F or gas 6
(200 deg C).
2. Roll out pastry and cut to line
four 4-inch (10-cm) diameter patty
tins. Bring pastry well up the
sides of each tin.
3. Prick base of each and line
with foil and baking beans. Bake
blind in centre of oven for 10
minutes.
4. Remove foil and baking beans
and cook for a further 5–10
minutes, then reduce oven
temperature to moderate, 350 deg
F or gas 4 (180 deg C).
5. Place a few slices of salami in
each flan case.
6. Blend together remaining
ingredients, except for lettuce
leaves and olives, and spoon over
salami.
7. Bake in centre of oven for
20–25 minutes, until filling is set.
8. Garnish with lettuce leaves,
black olives and extra slices of
salami and serve at once.

ITALIAN SCONES
Serves 4–6

1lb (½ kilo) plain flour
1oz (25gm) baking powder
1 teaspoon salt
1 stock cube
4oz (100gm) butter
1oz (25gm) cheese, grated
milk to mix
8oz (200gm) pork sausagemeat
4oz (100gm) Lancashire cheese
tomato slices or olives to
garnish

1. Preheat oven to hot, 425 deg F
or gas 7 (220 deg C).
2. Sieve the flour, baking powder
and salt together.
3. Crumble in the stock cube and
rub in the butter.
4. Add the grated cheese and mix
to a soft dough with the milk.
5. Roll out the dough to a ½-inch
thickness and cut into circles
approximately 4 inches in
diameter and place on a baking
sheet.
6. Form the sausagemeat into the
same number of 4-inch circles as
the scones.
7. Bake the scones in the centre
of the oven for 5 minutes, then
place the sausagemeat circles on
the top and continue cooking for
a further 10 minutes.
8. Remove from the oven, crumble
the Lancashire cheese over and
place under the grill until brown.
9. Garnish with tomato slices or
olives and serve with watercress.

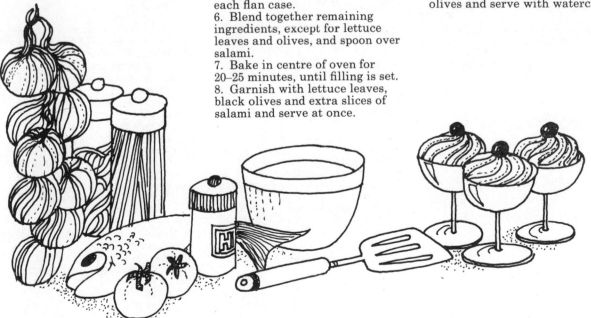

BITTERBALLEN
(Illustrated on page 17)
Makes 28–30

In Holland, *bitterballen* are served as an appetizer, and should be eaten piping hot. The sauce mixture may be made well in advance and kept in a refrigerator, but rolling them into small balls should be done an hour or two before the party. Ideally they should be served as soon as they have been fried and drained.

¼oz (6gm) powdered gelatine
½ pint (250ml) veal stock
1oz (25gm) butter
1oz (25gm) flour
6oz (150gm) cooked ham and veal, chopped
1 teaspoon chopped parsley
1oz (25gm) Gouda cheese, grated
seasoning
3oz (75gm) toasted breadcrumbs
1 small egg
fat for deep frying

1. Add gelatine to stock heating gently until thoroughly dissolved.
2. Make a white sauce using butter, flour and stock.
3. Add meat, parsley and cheese.
4. Season well, turn on to a plate and allow to cool until firm.
5. Roll into small balls, dip into breadcrumbs then into beaten egg and then into breadcrumbs again.
6. Fry in hot fat until golden brown, and drain on absorbent paper.
7. Serve in individual dishes on shredded lettuce.

COCKTAIL MEATBALLS
Makes 18–24

A Greek version – *keftedakia* – of the meatball appetizer.

1lb (½ kilo) minced steak
1 onion, finely grated
1–2 garlic cloves, crushed
salt and pepper
oregano
chopped mint
1–2 slices white bread
¼ pint (125ml) dry wine or water
1 egg
flour
olive oil
butter

1. Mix meat, onion, garlic, salt, pepper, oregano and mint.
2. Remove crusts from bread slices and moisten in wine or water.
3. Mix bread and egg into meat mixture.
4. Shape into 1-inch balls, dust with flour and fry, a few at a time, in equal amounts of olive oil and butter.
5. When meatballs are cooked and browned on all sides, drain and place immediately in casserole; cover and keep warm until ready to serve.

CHEESE BALLS
Serves 4

This recipe comes from St. Gall in Switzerland.

4 eggs, separated
10oz (250gm) cheese, grated
flour
fat for deep frying
tomato ketchup or sauce

1. Mix the egg yolks with the grated cheese.
2. Whip the egg whites and fold into the yolk mixture.
3. Shape mixture into walnut-size balls; roll them in flour.
4. Fry in deep fat, drain and serve very hot with tomato ketchup or sauce.

CHEESE PUDDING
Serves 4

From the traditional Dorrius restaurant in Amsterdam.

8oz (200gm) Gouda cheese, grated
½oz (12gm) butter
¼ pint (125ml) single cream
1 teaspoon made mustard
salt and pepper
1 egg, beaten

1. Preheat oven to moderate, 350 deg F or gas 4 (180 deg C).
2. Mix the cheese, butter, cream and mustard and season well with salt and pepper. Mix with the egg.
3. Place in a buttered ovenproof dish.
4. Bake in the centre of the oven for 20–25 minutes.
5. Serve hot.

EGG FLORENTINE WITH YOGURT TOPPING
Serves 4

1 packet (12oz or 300gm) frozen leaf spinach
6 eggs
salt and pepper
1oz (25gm) flour
2 cartons natural yogurt
1 level tablespoon grated Parmesan cheese
½ level teaspoon ground nutmeg

1. Preheat oven to moderate to moderately hot, 375 deg F or gas 5 (190 deg C).
2. Cook spinach according to instructions on the packet and drain well.
3. Divide between 4 greased cocotte dishes.
4. Make a well in the spinach and break 1 egg into each cocotte. Season well.
5. Mix together flour, yogurt and remaining eggs for topping and beat until smooth.
6. Divide mixture between cocottes, spooning carefully over the raw eggs.
7. Sprinkle with Parmesan cheese and nutmeg.
8. Bake in the centre of the oven for 10–25 minutes until topping is set.
9. Serve hot.

EMPRESS EGGS
Serves 4

A variation on eggs in cocotte dishes, from Holland, that makes an easily-prepared hors d'oeuvre.

2oz (50gm) butter
1 onion, chopped
4oz (100gm) cheese, grated
4 eggs

1. Preheat oven to moderate, 350 deg F or gas 4 (180 deg C).
2. Melt butter in shallow flameproof dish.
3. Fry onion to a golden brown and sprinkle with half of the cheese.
4. Break the eggs carefully over this mixture, taking care that they are evenly arranged and that the yolks remain whole.
5. Sprinkle remaining cheese over the eggs and bake in the centre of the oven until the whites are firm.

SPINACH AND EGG CANAPES
Serves 4

4 slices white bread, crusts removed
3oz (75gm) butter
1oz (25gm) flour
½ pint (250ml) milk
salt and pepper
4 hard-boiled eggs, chopped
1 small packet frozen spinach, cooked and well drained
chopped parsley to garnish

1. Fry bread in 2oz (50gm) of the butter; drain and cut in half diagonally.
2. Make a thick sauce with the remaining butter, the flour, milk, pepper and salt.
3. When cooked and thickened stir in the chopped hard-boiled eggs and spinach.
4. Spread mixture on fried bread slices and garnish with chopped parsley.

EGGS BAKED IN TOMATO PUREE
Serves 4

4 tablespoons tomato purée
4 eggs
butter
salt and pepper

1. Preheat oven to moderate, 350 deg F or gas 4 (180 deg C).
2. Heat tomato purée to boiling point and put 1 tablespoon into each of 4 individual buttered ramekin dishes.
3. Break an egg into each dish and add a few small pieces of butter.
4. Sprinkle with salt and pepper
5. Place in a pan of hot water so that the water level is half way up the ramekin dishes.
6. Cover with foil and greaseproof paper and bake in the centre of the oven until eggs are lightly set.
7. Serve with fingers of buttered toast.

FINNISH HERRING SALAD
Serves 4–6

2 herring fillets
10oz (250gm) carrot, cooked and chopped
2 large gherkins, chopped
1lb (½ kilo) beetroot, chopped
8oz (200gm) potatoes, cooked and chopped
2 apples, cored and chopped
2 hard-boiled eggs
1 carton soured or double cream
mustard
vinegar
sugar to taste
beetroot juice

1. Cut the herrings into small cubes.
2. Mix the prepared carrot, gherkins, beetroot, potatoes and apple in a bowl and toss lightly.
3. Sieve the egg yolk and chop the white and arrange, in strips, across the top of the salad.
4. Make a sharp-flavoured sauce with the cream, mustard, vinegar and sugar.
5. Colour the sauce a very pale pink with a few drops beetroot juice. Serve with the salad.

PICKLED SALT HERRING
Serves 4

A typical dish from a Swedish *smörgåsbord*, known as *inlagdsill*.

1 large salt herring
¼ pint (125ml) vinegar
2 tablespoons water
3oz (75gm) sugar
2oz (50gm) onion, chopped
5 peppercorns, crushed
10 whole allspice, crushed
2 sprigs fresh dill
fresh dill sprigs and raw onion rings to garnish

1. Clean herring, remove head. Rinse under cold running water
2. Soak in cold water 10–12 hours, changing water a few times so the herring will not be too salty.
3. Cut herring along backbone. Remove the big backbone and as many small ones as possible; pull off skin. (The bones come out easily after the soaking.)
4. Drain fillets on absorbent paper. Cut into thin slices with sharp knife and place in a long narrow dish.
5. Mix remaining ingredients together in a saucepan. Bring to the boil and simmer for a few minutes. Cool and strain.
6. Pour over herrings.
7. Garnish with a few sprigs of fresh dill and onion rings.
8. Cover dish with foil and refrigerate a few hours (or leave overnight) before serving.

SWEDISH HERRING SALAD
Serves 6–8

1 salt herring
1lb (½ kilo) potatoes, cooked
diced
1lb (½ kilo) pickled beetroots,
diced
2oz (50gm) gherkins, diced
3oz (75gm) apple, diced
1½oz (37gm) onion, finely
chopped
½ pint (250ml) vinegar or liquid
from pickled beetroots
2 tablespoons water
2 tablespoons sugar
pinch of pepper
hard-boiled egg slices and
chopped parsley to garnish

1. Clean fish and remove head.
Soak fish for 10–12 hours,
changing water a few times.
2. Bone and fillet as in the
previous recipe. Dice fillets.
3. Mix together the diced
ingredients. Add the herring.
4. Mix vinegar, water, sugar and
pepper; blend well.
5. Gently stir into fish mixture.
6. Pack into a dish that has been
rinsed in cold water or lightly
brushed with salad oil.
7. Chill in refrigerator a few
hours.
8. Turn on to a serving dish and
garnish with hard-boiled eggs and
chopped parsley. Serve with
soured cream.

CARELIAN PASTIES
Makes 20

A popular hors d'oeuvre dish
from Finland.

2 teaspoons salt
11oz (275gm) rye flour
½ pint (250ml) water
9oz (225gm) rice
3 pints (approximately 1½ litres)
milk
1 pint (approximately ½ litre)
water
melted butter (see method)
4 hard-boiled eggs, chopped

1. Preheat the oven to hot, 425
deg F or gas 7 (220 deg C).
2. Mix the salt and flour into a
stiff dough with water.
3. Work into a long roll and cut
into 20 equal pieces.
4. Shape these into balls and
flatten them on a floured board.
Roll into paper-thin rounds.
5. Meanwhile cook the rice until
soft in the milk and water.
6. To fill the pasties, place several
of the rounds on a board and put
1 tablespoon of the cooked rice in
the centre of each
7. Spread the rice evenly over the
pastry, leaving the sides
uncovered. Turn the sides to the
centre, but leave a narrow gap
down the middle. Form the edges
into small pleats, using the thumb
and forefinger. The pasties are
thus closed except for a thin
streak of filling which still
remains visible in the middle.
8. Place the pasties on baking
sheets and bake on the two top
shelves of the oven for about 20
minutes.
9. After baking, brush the pasties
with melted butter, to which has
been added a little boiling water
or cream.
10. Place the pasties on a plate in
twos and, if not serving
immediately, cover well with
greaseproof paper and a clean
teatowel.
11. Serve the pasties with
egg-butter – made from chopped
hard-boiled eggs mixed with a
little butter.

GREEK STUFFED TOMATOES
Serves 4–6

In Greece this dish is called
yemistes domates laderes.

12 tomatoes
salt and pepper
pinch of sugar
3 onions, grated
olive oil
3oz (75gm) parsley, chopped
3oz (75gm) dill, chopped
3½oz (87gm) raisins or currants
3½oz (87gm) pignolia or pine
nuts
6oz (150gm) long-grain rice
½ pint (250ml) water

1. Wash tomatoes, cut a slice off
the top of each and scoop out
pulp; save the tops.
1. Sprinkle inside of tomatoes
with salt, pepper and sugar.
3. Sauté onions in a little olive
oil until soft.
4. Mix onions, parsley, dill,
raisins or currants, pignolia or
pine nuts and rice with olive oil
to bind together fairly firmly.
Season to taste with salt and
pepper.
5. Fill tomatoes with this
mixture. Cover with tomato caps
and place in a fireproof dish with
remaining olive oil and the water.
6. Weight down tomatoes with a
heavy plate.
7. Cover dish and simmer for
about 30 minutes or until rice is
cooked.
8. Serve cold.

ZURICH MUSHROOM TARTLETS
Serves 4–6

5½oz (137gm) butter
7½oz (187gm) flour
1 egg
1 tablespoon salted water
1lb (½ kilo) mushrooms
2oz (50gm) onions, finely chopped
¼ pint (125ml) cream
salt and pepper
juice of 1 lemon

1. Preheat oven to moderate to moderately hot, 375 deg F or gas 5 (190 deg C).
2. Rub 4oz (100gm) of the butter into 7oz (175gm) of the flour and mix with the egg and water to form a dough.
3. Allow mixture to rest in a cool place for 30 minutes, then roll out the dough very thinly. Cut circles with a floured pastry cutter and use to line tartlet tins. Bake blind in the centre of the oven for 15–20 minutes.
4. Chop mushrooms, fry them in remaining butter; add the chopped onions and continue cooking until softened.
5. Add the remaining flour, stir, add the cream, season with salt and pepper, add lemon juice.
6. Simmer for 5 minutes, do not allow to boil. Take pastry shells from oven and fill with mushroom mixture. Serve very hot.

PITZ
Serves 4–6

This recipe comes from the Lower Valais area of Switzerland.

2lb (1 kilo) medium tomatoes
8oz (200gm) cheese
2 large onions
1 small bunch of fresh herbs
salt and pepper
shortcrust pastry made with 10oz (250gm) flour (see Basic recipes, page 100)
¼ pint (125ml) soured cream

1. Preheat oven to hot, 425 deg F or gas 7 (220 deg C).
2. Cut tomatoes in half, remove pips and cores.
3. Grate cheese finely, chop onions and herbs.
4. Mix together cheese and onions, season with salt and pepper and fill tomatoes with mixture.
5. Line a Swiss roll tin with pastry, place tomatoes in dish. Spoon a little soured cream over each tomato.
6. Bake in the centre of the oven for 30 minutes. Serve hot.

CHEESE TOAST A LA VAUDOISE
Serves 4

4 slices bread
butter
4 slices Gruyère cheese, ¼ inch thick
¼ pint (125ml) white wine
black pepper

1. Preheat oven to hot 425 deg F or gas 7 (220 deg C).
2. Spread one side of bread slices with butter.
2. Cover with a slice of Gruyère cheese, cutting it a little smaller than the bread.
3. Place in an ovenproof dish containing small pieces of butter and the wine.
4. Place in the oven until the cheese melts into a smooth paste.
5. Serve very hot sprinkled with freshly ground black pepper.

OVOS VERDES
Serves 4

An hors d'oeuvre dish from Portugal using eggs.

4 eggs
2 teaspoons minced onion
scant 2 teaspoons curry powder
2 tablespoons mayonnaise
2 heaped tablespoons finely chopped parsley
salt and pepper

1. Boil eggs for 10 minutes, plunge them into cold water for 10 minutes.
2. Remove shells, cut in half lengthwise and ease out yolks.
3. Mash yolks with the remaining ingredients and pile back into the egg whites.
4. Serve as part of a mixed hors d'oeuvre or with black olives, radishes and spring onions.

OEUFS MEULEMEESTER
Serves 6

A way of serving eggs, as an hors d'oeuvre, from Bruges.

6 eggs
2 teaspoons chopped chives
2 teaspoons chopped parsley
1 teaspoon French mustard
4oz (100gm) shelled prawns
2 cans (6oz or 150gm) cream
salt and pepper
4oz (100gm) soft cheese
2oz (50gm) butter
chopped parsley to garnish

1. Preheat oven to moderate to moderately hot, 400 deg F or gas 6 (200 deg C).
2. Boil eggs for 7 minutes.
3. Put into cold water for 2 minutes then peel and slice into a mixing bowl.
4. Add the chives, parsley, mustard, prawns, cream and salt and pepper.
5. Mix and pour into individual buttered ovenproof dishes.
6. Spoon cheese on top and dot with butter.
7. Bake in the centre of the oven for 10–15 minutes.
8. Serve at once, garnished with chopped parsley.

CHICORY AND EGGS DUTCH STYLE
Serves 4

A Dutch way of serving eggs as an hors d'oeuvre. In Holland this dish is known as *lofschotel*.

8 heads chicory
4 hard-boiled eggs
3oz (75gm) butter
nutmeg (optional)

1. Cook chicory in boiling salted water until tender, approximately 15 minutes, taking care that they remain whole.
2. Drain and place on a hot serving dish.
3. Garnish with halved hard-boiled eggs, and serve with creamed butter.
4. Nutmeg can be sprinkled over the dish if liked.

EGGS A LA FLAMENCA
Serves 6

1 large onion, peeled and chopped
2 cloves garlic, peeled and chopped
2 tablespoons oil
2oz (50gm) ham, chopped
6oz (150gm) garlic sausage
2oz (50gm) cooked peas
2oz (50gm) cooked French beans
2 red and green peppers, de-seeded and sliced
salt and pepper
6 eggs
1 teaspoon chopped parsley

1. Preheat oven to moderate, 350 deg F or gas 4 (180 deg C).
2. Fry the onion and garlic in the oil until soft
3. Add the ham, sausage, peas, beans and half the peppers.
4. Fry for about 5 minutes. Season to taste.
5. Spoon the mixture into a shallow ovenproof dish and make six hollows with the back of a spoon. Into each hollow break an egg.
6. Sprinkle with the parsley and top with the remaining slices of pepper.
7. Bake in the centre of the oven for 25–35 minutes or until the eggs are set.
8. Serve hot.

DUTCH POTATO ROLLS
Serves 4–6

This dish is known as *aardappel broadjes* in Holland.

2lb (1 kilo) mashed potatoes
milk
butter
salt and pepper
nutmeg
3 egg yolks
2 tablespoons tomato purée
2oz (50gm) ham, finely chopped
butter for frying

1. Cream mashed potatoes with milk, butter, seasoning and nutmeg to taste.
2. Remove from heat and add the egg yolks, tomato purée and chopped ham.
3. With floured hands, shape into small rolls and fry in butter until golden brown all over.
4. Drain on absorbent paper and serve hot.

DUTCH CHEESE CROQUETTES
Makes 12

½ pint (250ml) white sauce (see Basic recipes, page 100)
8oz (200gm) Gouda cheese, grated
2 egg yolks
1 heaped tablespoon chopped chives
salt and pepper
dash of Worcestershire sauce
2 egg whites
browned breadcrumbs

1. Make a white sauce with 2oz (50gm) flour and ½ pint (250ml) milk and bring to the boil stirring continuously.
2. Add the cheese, egg yolks, chives and seasoning, stir until smooth and of a thick creamy consistency.
3. Turn on to a dish and put in a cool place until really firm – preferably overnight.
4. Shape into 12 croquettes
5. Coat with beaten egg white and breadcrumbs twice.
6. Fry in deep fat until golden brown, drain on kitchen paper.
7. Serve hot at once, with mixed vegetables or salad.

ASPARAGUS HAM AU GRAS
Serves 6

1 can (1lb or ½ kilo) green asparagus spears, drained
8oz (200gm) cooked ham, cubed
8oz (200gm) boiled long-grain rice (raw weight)
1 teaspoon salt
1 teaspoon black pepper
1 teaspoon cayenne pepper
2oz (50gm) canned pimento, chopped
½ teaspoon dry mustard
4oz (100gm) Gruyère cheese, grated
¼ pint (125ml) plus 5 tablespoons double cream, whipped

1. Preheat oven to moderate, 350 deg F or gas 4 (180 deg C).
2. Arrange asparagus in a buttered ovenproof dish.
3. Place ham over asparagus.
4. Season rice with salt, pepper and cayenne pepper.
5. Add pimento and toss lightly. Spoon over ham.
6. Add dry mustard and cheese to the whipped cream.
7. Spread over top of rice.
8. Bake in centre of the oven for 30 minutes.
9. Serve hot.

MALINES ASPARAGUS SOUFFLE
Serves 4

An asparagus soufflé recipe from Belgium.

1lb (½ kilo) asparagus
melted butter
1 large onion, chopped
6oz (150gm) butter
4 hard-boiled egg yolks
parsley
salt and pepper

1. Remove the hard asparagus ends and leave the stalks in some melted butter mixed with chopped onion for 30 minutes.
2. Remove and cook in boiling salted water until just tender.
3. Drain well and serve as follows: each guest makes their own sauce for the asparagus by crushing the egg yolk in a little of the butter and sprinkling it with parsley, salt and pepper.

Country herring terrine (see page 8)   Mushrooms with cream (see page 8)
Individual salami and cottage cheese quiches (see page 11)   Bitterballen (see page 12)

Dutch pea soup (see page 24)   Gazpacho (see page 28)

Cold raspberry soup (see page 29)   Cucumber and yogurt salad (see page 32)

BRIGITTE'S TOMATOES
Serves 3–6

6 large tomatoes
3oz (75gm) butter
1 small onion, finely chopped
½ garlic clove, finely chopped
2oz (50gm) streaky bacon,
chopped
1oz (25gm) mushrooms,
chopped
2oz (50gm) fresh breadcrumbs
salt and pepper

1. Preheat oven to moderate, 350 deg F or gas 4 (180 deg C).
2. Slice the top off each tomato, remove pulp with a teaspoon.
3. Melt 2oz (50gm) butter in a pan and lightly fry onion and garlic.
4. Add bacon and mushrooms and cook until tender. Remove from heat.
5. Stir in breadcrumbs and season well. Fill each of the tomatoes with some of this mixture.
6. Spread ½oz (12gm) butter on the base of a shallow ovenproof dish.
7. Put the tomatoes, close together, into the dish. Dot remaining butter on stuffing and replace tomato lids.
8. Bake in centre of the oven for about 20 minutes.

ALGARVE OYSTERS
Serves 4

24 large fresh oysters
butter
chopped parsley
2 dessertspoons white wine
salt and pepper
fresh breadcrumbs

1. Preheat oven to very moderate, 325 deg F or gas 3 (170 deg C).
2. Wash the oysters well.
3. Place in a saucepan over heat to make them open.
4. Remove from their shell and allow them to soak in their own liquid.
5. Bring to the boil for 2–3 minutes.
6. Grease an ovenproof dish with butter and arrange the oysters, in layers, with chopped parsley, white wine, salt and pepper.
7. Add plenty of butter and sprinkle breadcrumbs on the top.
8. Cook in the centre of the oven until the crumbs are browned and oysters heated through.

JANSEN'S TEMPTATIONS
Serves 4

4oz (100gm) butter
2 medium onions, thinly sliced
2lb (1 kilo) old potatoes, peeled and thinly sliced
2 pickled herring fillets, thinly sliced
1 can (2oz or 50gm) anchovy fillets, drained
salt and pepper
¼ pint (125ml) single cream

1. Preheat oven to moderate to moderately hot, 375 deg F or gas 5 (190 deg C).
2. Melt 2oz (50gm) of the butter and lightly fry onions.
3. Use half the remaining butter to grease a 2-pint (approximately 1-litre) ovenproof dish.
4. Layer potatoes, onions, herrings and anchovies in the dish, finishing with a layer of potatoes. Season and dot surface with remaining butter.
5. Cover and bake in the centre of the oven for 1½ hours, or until potatoes are cooked.
6. Remove from oven, pour single cream over potatoes, then serve.

NORWEGIAN HERRING ROE PATE
Serves 6

1 can (8oz or 200gm) soft herring roes or use fresh herring roes
2 level teaspoons plain flour
6oz (150gm) butter, melted
1 tablespoon lemon juice
good pinch each of nutmeg and black pepper
pinch of salt
2 level teaspoons finely chopped parsley

1. Drain canned herring roes, toss in flour.
2. Heat 2oz (50gm) butter in a pan and gently fry roes for about 5 minutes, turning, until they begin to break up.
3. Remove from heat and beat well to make a smooth paste (or blend in a liquidizer).
4. Gradually beat in remaining butter, the lemon juice, nutmeg and seasonings. Finally, stir in parsley and turn pâté into a small dish.
5. Cover and chill until ready to use. Serve with warm toast.

HERRINGS IN TOMATO
Serves 4

This dish is known as *tomatstromming* in Norway, where it originated.

1¾lb (700gm) herring or sprats
6 tablespoons oil
2 tablespoons vinegar
2 tablespoons tomato purée
1–1½ teaspoons salt
½ saltspoon white pepper

1. Clean the herring and remove the backbones. Wash well and drain.
2. Pack the herrings, closely together, in a fireproof dish.
3. Mix the rest of the ingredients to make a dressing.
4. Pour over the herrings, cover and simmer for about 7–8 minutes. Allow to cool in the liquid.
5. Serve when quite cold.

PORTUGUESE TUNA AND CUCUMBER PANCAKES
Serves 4

½ pint (250ml) pancake batter (see Basic recipes, page 100)
oil for frying
1 can (7oz or 175gm) tuna fish, drained
4 tablespoons natural yogurt
½ pint (250ml) white sauce (see Basic recipes, page 100)
4 tablespoons grated cucumber
pinch of nutmeg
toasted breadcrumbs

1. Preheat oven to moderate, 350 deg F or gas 4 (180 deg C).
2. Make the pancakes in the usual way, frying them in a little oil.
3. Fill each one with a mixture of tuna mashed with yogurt.
4. Roll up and arrange in an ovenproof dish.
5. Make the white sauce and add the cucumber and nutmeg.
6. Pour sauce over the pancakes.
7. Sprinkle with breadcrumbs.
8. Cook in the centre of the oven for 20 minutes.
9. Serve hot.

SWISS FONDUE
Serves 4

One way to open a dinner party or for a meal on its own (these amounts are enough for a main course). Ideally, to serve fondue, you need a fondue set.

1 clove garlic
8–12oz (200–300gm) Gruyère cheese
8–12oz (200–300gm) Emmental cheese
2–4 level teaspoons cornflour or white flour
⅓–½ bottle dry white wine
few drops lemon juice
1 small glass Kirsch
freshly ground black pepper
grated nutmeg

1. Rub a fondue dish with the cut garlic clove.
2. Grate the Gruyère and the Emmental cheese into the fondue dish. Add the flour, wine and lemon juice.
3. Bring to the boil, stirring all the while. Remove from the heat and add the Kirsch, a sprinkling of pepper and a little nutmeg.
4. Keep the fondue hot during the meal over a very low flame and serve with cubes of French bread or, if liked, small cubes of raw vegetables. Each guest spears a piece of bread on a long-handled fork and dips it into the fondue.
5. If the fondue should separate, place the pan back on the heat and add a few drops of lemon juice; bring the fondue back to the boil, stirring vigorously.

CHEESE FONDUE
Serves 6–8

Another version of the Swiss dish using canned soup as a base.

2 garlic cloves
1lb (½ kilo) Emmental cheese, grated
½ pint (250ml) white wine
½oz (12gm) cornflour
1 tablespoon Kirsch
1 can (15½oz or 387gm) cream of celery soup
French bread cubes

1. Peel the garlic, rub it around the inside of a saucepan, then crush it.
2. Place the cheese and crushed garlic in the saucepan and add the wine.
3. Slowly melt the cheese over a low heat. Stir in the wine.
4. Blend the cornflour and Kirsch together and add to the melted cheese mixture.
5. Bring to the boil, stirring, to thicken the mixture, cook for a few minutes then lower the heat.
6. Add the celery soup, gradually, stirring well between additions.
7. This fondue can be kept warm over a low heat but should not be allowed to boil again.
8. Serve with French bread cubes for dipping into the fondue.

SWISS CHEESE FONDUE WITH RICE BALLS
Serves 4–6

Rice balls are substituted for French bread in this recipe.

2 eggs, beaten
8oz (200gm) boiled long-grain rice (raw weight)
12 cheese-flavoured crackers, crushed
2 tablespoons minced onion
1 tablespoon minced parsley
3oz (75gm) melted butter or margarine
1 garlic clove, peeled
1lb (½ kilo) Gruyère cheese, grated
1½oz (37gm) flour
¾ pint (375ml) white wine
1 teaspoon salt
pinch of white pepper
dash of nutmeg
6 tablespoons Kirsch

1. Preheat oven to hot, 450 deg F of gas 8 (230 deg C).
2. Combine the eggs, rice, crackers, onion, parsley and melted fat for rice balls and mix well.
3. Chill for 30 minutes.
4. Form into 40 1-inch balls.
5. Place in a baking tin and cook in the centre of the oven for 15 minutes until lightly browned.
6. To prepare fondue, rub garlic over bottom of a fondue dish.
7. Mix cheese and flour.
8. Heat wine until almost boiling.
9. Add cheese gradually, stirring constantly.
10. Add salt, pepper and nutmeg.
11. Slowly add Kirsch and continue stirring until mixture is well blended.
12. When mixture boils, serve at once, keeping fondue hot over a low flame. Serve with the rice balls.

FRENCH BREAD DUNKS WITH CHEESE FONDUE SAUCE
Serves 4

A third variation on a Swiss fondue theme.

1lb (½ kilo) Gruyère or
Emmental cheese, grated
1½oz (37gm) flour
1 pint (approximately ½ litre)
white wine
pinch of ground nutmeg
1 garlic clove, chopped
½ teaspoon Tabasco sauce
½ teaspoon salt
freshly ground black pepper
2 French loaves, cut in pieces

1. Combine cheese and flour and mix until grated cheese is well coated with flour.
2. Pour wine into pan and cook over low heat until beginning to bubble.
3. Stir in cheese a little at a time and continue stirring until cheese is thoroughly melted and the mixture bubbles.
4. Add nutmeg, garlic, Tabasco sauce and seasoning to taste.
5. To serve dip pieces of French bread into sauce.

FRENCH CHICKEN LIVER PATE
Serves 4

4oz (100gm) butter
1 medium onion, finely
chopped
8oz (200gm) chicken livers
1 dessertspoon French mustard
2 tablespoons brandy
1 tablespoon port

1. Melt the butter and sauté the onion until soft.
2. Chop the livers, add to the pan and fry quickly over a brisk heat, until just browned; do not overcook.
3. Rub through a sieve, or blend in a liquidizer. Add the other ingredients and blend or beat until smooth.
4. Check seasoning. Turn into individual pots, chill and serve with hot toast.

POLISH PIEROGI STUFFED WITH HAM
Makes about 18

4oz (100gm) self-raising flour
salt
1 egg yolk
little cold water
1 small onion
2oz (50gm) butter
2oz (50gm) ham or boiled bacon,
chopped
pinch of mixed herbs
salt and pepper
crisp breadcrumbs

1. Sift the flour with salt into a bowl. Mix with egg yolk and enough cold water to make a firm dough.
2. Knead lightly and roll out fairly thinly and cut into 2-inch squares. Brush edges with egg white.
3. Chop onion, fry in half the butter until tender. Mix with the ham, herbs and seasoning (add the butter from pan).
4. Put small heaps of filling on the pastry squares, fold over into triangle shapes.
5. Seal edges very firmly by pressing with a fork both sides.
6. Drop pastry squares into boiling salted water. When they are cooked they rise to the surface.
8. Remove and arrange in a heated dish. Sprinkle with crisp breadcrumbs and top with remaining butter, melted. Serve at once.

BERLIN ROLLMOPS
Serves 6

These are often eaten in Berlin as a 'morning after' snack; also served as an hors d'oeuvre.

6 herrings
2oz (50gm) salt
1 pint (approximately ½ litre)
water
1 pint (approximately ½ litre)
vinegar
1 tablespoon pickling spice
12 gherkins
2 small onions, peeled and very
thinly sliced
2–3 bayleaves
2 dried chilli peppers

1. Clean the herrings, discard the head and fins and remove the backbone. Cut each herring in

two and soak in the salt and water for 1 hour.
2. Drain and dry well. Place in a shallow dish, cover with half the vinegar and set aside for 3–4 hours.
3. Meanwhile, boil the remaining vinegar with the pickling spice; set aside to cool, then strain.
4. Drain the herrings, and roll up each fillet with a gherkin and a thin onion ring inside. Secure with a cocktail stick if necessary.
5. Place in a jar or bowl and cover with the prepared vinegar.
6. Add the bayleaves and chilli peppers.
7. Cover and serve when required. (In a cool place the herrings will keep for about 1 month.)

ESCABECHE SAUCE (FOR FISH)

A popular Portuguese summer hors d'oeuvre is cold cooked fish covered with escabeche sauce. Mackerel fillets are usually used, but other varieties of fish can be treated in the same way.

3 onions, sliced
olive oil
1 garlic clove, finely chopped
1 bayleaf
2 tablespoons white vinegar

1. Fry the onions until dark golden brown in olive oil with garlic and the bayleaf.
2. Fry fish separately.
3. When onions are ready, remove from heat and add vinegar. Add the fish.
4. Cover the pan and leave to get cold.
5. The fish can be kept for up to a week in the refrigerator in the escabeche sauce. This sauce should not be served until it has been kept in the refrigerator for at least two days for the flavours to blend.

Soups and salads

Recipes for hearty soups for cold weather and delicately-flavoured, chilled soups for summer days can be found here, as well as appetising ideas for presenting salads.

In Europe, soups can be a whole meal such as bowls of goulash soup taken with glasses of wine in German wine *Stubes*, as in Heidelberg. Soups may be a vast bowl of mixed fish eaten at fishermen's cafes in the old port areas – the *bouillabaise* of Southern France for example and similar soups will be found in Spain and Portugal.

In Holland, thick pea soup keeps out the cold mists that creep in from the sea; in Italy minestrone is substantiated with the addition of pasta. By contrast there are the chilled summer soups of Spain, led by the somewhat fiery gazpacho, the lighter lemon soups of Greece and the unique fruit soups of strawberries and raspberries that are delightful on a hot summer day.

Soups are often based on necessity; made from a handful of what is to hand. So bortsch became a peasants' dish in Russia, in Portugal the bread soups (*açorda*) were the food of beggars who kept bread scraps and added garlic and water to them; now they are much refined with added meats.

Salads, too, were often a mélange of local items to hand and are much more substantial and appealing than our soggy lettuce and tomato affairs. In Greece there is the salad with *feta* cheese and olives; in other countries vegetables are cooled with soured cream or yogurt, and lots of mixed vegetables are made more substantial with rice or pasta. Fish is also added to salads – herrings in the north, anchovies in southern France and tuna fish in Italy.

AUSTRIAN VEGETABLE SOUP
Serves 4–6

Many Continental soups, such as this one, are rich vegetable mixtures.

1oz (25gm) butter
2oz (50gm) fine semolina
¾ pint (375ml) chicken stock
1 medium onion, chopped
2 carrots, grated
several spring green leaves, shredded
pinch of mixed herbs
1 pint (approximately ½ litre) milk
1 carton (5oz or 125gm) natural yogurt
salt and pepper
chopped chives or parsley to garnish

1. Melt the butter, add semolina and cook over a low heat for 2 minutes, stirring. Stir in the stock and simmer for 15 minutes.
2. Add onion, carrots, greens and herbs to taste.
3. Simmer for 10 minutes and remove from heat.
4. Whisk in the milk and yogurt and heat gently without boiling.
5. Season to taste.
6. Serve sprinkled with chopped parsley or chives.

FRENCH COUNTRY SOUP
Serves 4

6oz (150gm) streaky bacon, de-rinded
1 tablespoon oil
1lb (½ kilo) onions
1lb (½ kilo) potatoes
1 can (14oz or 350gm) tomatoes
1 pint (approximately ½ litre) chicken stock
pinch ground mace
1 carton (5oz or 125gm) soured cream

1. Cut the bacon into ½-inch pieces and fry in oil in large saucepan, until crisp and golden brown. Drain and keep on one side.
2. Chop onions roughly, add to pan and cook gently for 2–3 minutes until soft.
3. Peel potatoes and slice thinly. Add to onions together with tomatoes, stock, mace and half the bacon.
4. Bring to boil and simmer gently for 1 hour with lid on pan.
5. Rub the soup through a sieve or blend in a liquidizer. Return to the pan.
6. Stir in half the soured cream. (If soup is too thick, add extra water to make pouring consistency.)
7. Reheat but do not boil. Pour into individual bowls. Sprinkle with remaining bacon and spoon soured cream into centre of each. Serve immediately.

MINESTRONE
Serves 4–6

3–4oz (75–100gm) ham fore end,
cut into matchstick strips
1oz (25gm) butter
1 medium onion, chopped
2 garlic cloves, chopped
2 tomatoes, peeled and chopped
½ teaspoon dried basil
1 stick celery, chopped
1–1½ pints (approximately ½–¾
litre) stock
2 potatoes, peeled and diced
½ red pepper, thinly sliced
½ green pepper, thinly sliced
1 courgette, sliced
4oz (100gm) macaroni
salt and pepper
grated Parmesan cheese

1. Fry the ham in the butter until
lightly browned.
2. Add the onion and garlic and
cook until transparent.
3. Add the tomatoes, basil and
celery and cook for 8–10 minutes
stirring frequently.
4. Add the stock and potatoes and
simmer for 5 minutes.
5. Add the peppers, courgette and
macaroni. Simmer for 7–8 minutes
or until all are tender.
6. Season to taste with salt and
pepper and serve hot with grated
Parmesan cheese.

QUICK MINESTRONE SOUP
Serves 4

A time saving way of making the
favourite soup of Italy using
convenience foods.

½oz (12gm) margarine
1 small onion, finely chopped
1 garlic clove, crushed
1 pint (approximately ½ litre)
water
8oz (200gm) frozen mixed
vegetables
4oz (100gm) cabbage or celery,
finely shredded
1 packet (1 pint or
approximately ½ litre) chicken
noodle soup
2 tomatoes, skinned and
coarsely chopped
salt and pepper

1. Melt the margarine in a large
saucepan, add the onion and
garlic and fry gently for 2
minutes.
2. Add the water, boil and then
add the mixed vegetables and
cabbage or celery.
3. Bring back to the boil and
cook gently for 5 minutes.
4. Add the chicken noodle soup
and tomatoes and simmer for a
further 5 minutes.
5. Season to taste. Serve hot.

DUTCH VERMICELLI SOUP WITH MEATBALLS
Serves 6

2 blades mace
2 pints (approximately 1 litre)
stock
4oz (100gm) lean minced beef
salt and pepper
grated nutmeg
flour
2oz (50gm) fine vermicelli
chopped parsley to garnish

1. Add mace to the stock, bring
to the boil and simmer for 15
minutes.
2. Season the meat with salt,
pepper and nutmeg and shape into
small balls about the size of
marbles.
3. Roll meatballs in flour and add
to the soup.
4. Crush the vermicelli lightly,
add to the soup, cover and simmer
for 20 minutes.
5. Remove the mace blades,
garnish with chopped parsley and
serve at once.

CZECHOSLOVAKIAN ONION SOUP
Serves 6

4 large onions, thickly sliced
3½ pints (approximately 1¾
litres) beef stock
4 eggs, beaten
4 slices rye bread
4oz (100gm) cooking fat

1. Simmer the onions in the stock
until tender.
2. Add the beaten eggs.
3. Bring just to the boil and pour
into a hot serving dish.
4. Sprinkle with the slices of rye
bread cut into strips and fried in
the fat.

FRENCH ONION SOUP
Serves 4–6

2oz (50gm) margarine
1lb (½ kilo) onions, sliced
½ teaspoon salt
pinch of brown sugar
1½ pints (approximately ¾ litre)
beef stock
4 slices French bread
2oz (50gm) cheese, grated

1. Melt half the fat in pan. Cook
onions very gently until golden
and transparent.
2. Add salt and a pinch of brown
sugar.
3. Pour on hot beef stock and
simmer gently for 20–30 minutes.
4. Fry the slices of bread, on both
sides, in the remaining margarine.
Drain.
5. Sprinkle with grated cheese
and place in the bottom of a hot
soup bowl.
6. Pour soup over and cover for
3–4 minutes to soften bread before
serving with extra grated cheese.

CREME DUBARRY DE FINISTERRE
Serves 4

1½oz (37gm) butter
1lb (½ kilo) cauliflower florets
4oz (100gm) white parts of leeks
bouquet garni
1½oz (37gm) flour
1½ pints (approximately ¾ litre) veal bone stock
4 tablespoons milk
salt and pepper
1 egg yolk
¼ pint (125ml) fresh cream
little dry white wine
small cauliflower florets to garnish

1. Preheat oven to very moderate, 325 deg F or gas 3 (170 deg C).
2. Melt butter, add cauliflower florets, leeks and bouquet garni. Fry for 2–3 minutes, but do not brown; remove from heat.
3. Add flour, mix well and cook in the centre of the oven for 10 minutes; do *not* allow to brown. Allow to cool.
4. Mix in, a little at a time, the hot veal stock, add milk, salt and pepper to taste, and simmer for 30 minutes.
5. Remove from heat and press through sieve, or blend in a liquidizer. Return to the pan and reheat.
6. Mix egg yolk and cream and add to soup with the wine (do not boil).
7. Serve garnished with small cauliflower florets.

GERMAN GOULASH SOUP
Serves 6–8

A quick way of making this traditional German soup using packet seasoning mixes.

3 pints (approximately 1½ litres) water
1 packet beef stew seasoning mix
1 medium onion, chopped
1 teaspoon seasoned salt
2½–3lb (1¼–1½ kilo) shin of beef on the bone
little flour (optional)

1. Place the water in a large saucepan.
2. Add the beef stew seasoning mix, chopped onion and seasoned salt. Stir thoroughly.
3. Add the beef. Bring to the boil, reduce heat, cover and simmer for about 2½ hours, until meat is very tender.
4. Remove meat and bone from soup stock and chop meat into small pieces.
5. Return meat to the soup.
6. Thicken soup with flour and water mixture, if wished and simmer for about another 20 minutes.

DUTCH PEA SOUP
(Illustrated on page 18)
Serves 6

A very popular soup in Holland where it is often served as a main course.

8oz (200gm) dried split peas
3 pints (approximately 1½ litres) water
2 pig's trotters
1 marrow bone
salt and pepper
8oz (200gm) potatoes, peeled and sliced
3 leeks, sliced
3 sticks celery, sliced
3 onions, sliced
chopped parsley
4 frankfurter sausages

1. Wash the peas and soak them in half the water overnight.
2. Simmer trotters and marrow bone in remaining water for 1 hour.
3. Add the peas plus the soaking water. Cook until soft, about 1 hour. Season well.
4. Add the potatoes, leeks, celery and onions and cook for a further 40 minutes.
5. Remove the marrow bone and trotters, scrape out the meat and return this to the soup.
6. If necessary thin the soup with a little stock. Adjust seasoning.
7. Stir in parsley and sliced frankfurters, allow to heat and serve.

SWEDISH PEA SOUP WITH PORK
Serves 4

The pork cooked in this soup is sliced and served with mustard, at the same time as the soup.

1¼lb (500gm) dried yellow peas
5 pints (approximately 2½ litres) water
1lb (½ kilo) lightly salted belly of pork or 2lb (1 kilo) shoulder with bone
2 medium onions, sliced
½ teaspoon ginger
1 teaspoon marjoram
salt and pepper

1. Rinse the peas. Place in a saucepan, add water and soak overnight. Do not change water.
2. Place over high heat and bring quickly to the boil – remove any shells floating on top. Cover and simmer about 2 hours.
3. Add pork, onions and seasonings except salt and pepper. Cover and simmer gently until pork and peas are tender, about 1 hour.
4. Add salt and pepper. Remove pork.
5. Serve the soup in bowls and cut the pork into slices and serve separately, with mustard.

LUXEMBOURG GREEN BEAN SOUP
Serves 4

8oz (200gm) green beans, sliced
4oz (100gm) potatoes, diced
4oz (100gm) onion, chopped
water to cover
salt and pepper
4 bacon rashers
½ pint (250ml) double or soured cream

1. Cover beans, potatoes and onion with water. Cook until vegetables are soft. Season to taste.
2. Fry the bacon until very crisp. Crumble and add pieces to the soup.
3. Add the cream and simmer (do not boil) for a few moments. Serve.

LUXEMBOURG POTATO SOUP
Serves 4–6

4–5 leeks (white parts only), chopped
2oz (50gm) butter
4–5 medium potatoes, diced
1½ pints (approximately ¾ litre) boiling water
salt and pepper
1½ pints (approximately ¾ litre) milk
2 egg yolks
¼ pint (125ml) double or soured cream

1. Wash leeks well and cook slowly in half the butter over low heat until transparent and soft.
2. Add potatoes with boiling water and seasoning to taste.
3. Simmer for 30 minutes. Rub through sieve or blend in a liquidizer.
4. Return to heat. Add hot milk, stir constantly and add the rest of the butter.
5. Add the egg yolks beaten with the cream. Reheat, but do not boil.

PARMENTIER SOUP
Serves 8

The classic French potato soup.

2oz (50gm) butter
1lb (½ kilo) potatoes, peeled and sliced
3 leeks (white parts only), chopped
1½ pints (approximately ¾ litre) stock
salt and pepper
¼ pint (125ml) double cream
¼ pint (125ml) milk
chopped chives to garnish

1. Melt half the butter and fry the vegetables for 3–4 minutes.
2. Add stock, salt and pepper, bring to the boil, cover and simmer for 40 minutes.
3. Rub through a sieve or blend in a liquidizer. Return to saucepan, adjust seasoning and reheat.
4. Add rest of butter, the cream and milk; reheat, but do not allow to boil.
5. Sprinkle with chives before serving.

POTATO SOUP
Serves 4

A popular Italian soup called *zuppa di patata*.

1lb (½ kilo) potatoes
1 large onion
2 sticks celery
1oz (25gm) butter
¾ pint (375ml) water
seasoning
1oz (25gm) cornflour
½ pint (250ml) milk
2 tablespoons chopped parsley to garnish

1. Peel and slice the potatoes.
2. Thinly slice the onion and celery.
3. Fry vegetables very gently in butter in a saucepan for 10 minutes. Do not allow to brown.
4. Add water and seasoning.
5. Bring to boil. Simmer for 45 minutes.
6. Rub through a sieve or blend in a liquidizer. Return to the pan.
7. Mix cornflour to a paste with a little of the milk.
8. Stir in remaining milk and blended cornflour.
9. Bring to boil, stirring.
10. Sprinkle with parsley and serve.

SPANISH LENTIL SOUP
Serves 4–6

The weather can be cold up in the Sierras in winter, so the Spanish make this a complete meal for cold days with fingers of bread fried in olive oil.

8oz (200gm) lentils
¼ pint (125ml) olive oil
1 large onion, finely chopped
chopped parsley
salt and black pepper
½oz (12gm) flour (optional)

1. Soak lentils overnight in water.
2. Drain and boil in 2½ pints (approximately 1¼ litres) slightly salted water for about 2 hours, or until soft.
3. Strain and reserve liquid. In a pan reheat lentils in olive oil.
4. Add lentil stock, onion, parsley and salt and pepper.
5. Simmer for 15 minutes, stirring occasionally.
6. Thicken soup (if liked) with flour, in the usual way.

BORTSCH
Serves 4

A traditional Russian soup.

2 medium onions
1 tablespoon oil
3 medium beetroots
6oz (150gm) cabbage
1¼ pints (625ml) stock
2 tablespoons vinegar
¼ level teaspoon salt
pepper
1 carton (5oz or 125gm) soured cream

1. Chop onions finely and cook gently in oil in large saucepan until soft, about 7 minutes.
2. Remove outside skin from beetroot, chop roughly and add to onions.
3. Shred cabbage finely and add to onions and beetroot.
4. Add stock, vinegar, salt and pepper.
5. Bring to boil and simmer for 1 hour with lid on pan.
6. Rub through a sieve or blend in a liquidizer.
7. Return to pan and reheat. If soup is too thick, add water to make a pouring consistency.
8. Pour into soup bowls and place a spoonful of soured cream in centre of each. Serve immediately.

CZECH SOUR SOUP WITH MUSHROOMS
Serves 6

4 potatoes, diced
2 pints (approximately 1 litre) beef stock
4oz (100gm) mushrooms
pinch of caraway or cumin seeds
salt
½ pint (250ml) soured cream
1oz (25gm) flour
6 eggs
chopped parsley or chives to garnish

1. Boil potatoes in the beef stock with the sliced mushrooms, a pinch of caraway or cumin seeds and salt.
2. When the potatoes are almost soft, add the soured cream mixed with the flour.
3. Season to taste.
4. Gently simmer the soup with the cream (do not boil); break in the eggs.
5. Simmer for 5–7 minutes.
6. Sprinkle with chopped parsley or chives and serve.

SWISS CHEESE SOUP
Serves 4

7oz (175gm) stale brown bread
9½oz (237gm) Swiss cheese
2 pints (approximately 1 litre) water
salt
¼ pint (125ml) dry white wine

1. Cut bread and cheese into small thin slices, place in a large soup tureen, alternating layers.
2. Cover with boiling water and leave to stand for 2–3 hours.
3. Pour the mixture into a saucepan, add salt bring to the boil and crush ingredients with a wooden spoon.
4. Stir well, add wine and serve.

FINNISH SUMMER SOUP
Serves 4–6

½ tablespoon sugar
1 tablespoon salt
1 pint (approximately ½ litre) water
2 carrots
8oz (200gm) garden peas
1 small cauliflower
1lb (½ kilo) potatoes, sliced
1 pint (approximately ½ litre) hot milk
few fresh spinach leaves
2oz (50gm) butter
chopped parsley to garnish

1. Mix the sugar and salt with water in a saucepan.
2. When the water is boiling, cut the carrots in thin slices and add to the water.
3. Add the peas, cauliflower, cut in pieces, potatoes, hot milk and spinach torn in small pieces. Allow to simmer for about 15 minutes.
4. Before serving, dot the top with butter and garnish with chopped parsley.

ITALIAN TOMATO CONSOMME
Serves 3

A quick way of enlivening canned consommé soup.

1 can consommé
3 tablespoons dry sherry
1 can (5½oz or 137gm) tomato juice
1 level teaspoon tomato purée
few drops lemon juice
chopped parsley and cooked noodles to garnish

1. Mix all the ingredients together except the parsley and noodles.
2. Heat through, check the seasoning and serve garnished with chopped parsley and noodles.

AVGOLEMONO SOUP
Serves 4–6

A delicious light and tangy Greek soup.

1 small chicken
8oz (200gm) long-grain rice
3–5 eggs
1 teaspoon lemon juice
freshly ground black pepper

1. Simmer the chicken and rice with water to cover until the meat is practically falling off the bones.
2. Beat the eggs in a large bowl with the lemon juice.
3. Pour the chicken liquid on to the eggs *very* slowly, the smallest amount at a time and whisking all the time.
4. When the amount in the bowl is double that of the originally beaten eggs, pour it back into a clean pan. Add the remaining broth and the chicken meat taken from the bones.
5. Reheat, but do not boil and serve sprinkled with freshly ground black pepper. The Greeks often sprinkle on a little powdered cinnamon too.

LEMON CHICKEN SOUP
Serves 4–6

A quick variation of the Greek *avgolémono*, without the rice, which is served cold.

2 cans (15oz or 375gm) clear chicken broth
3 eggs
grated rind and juice of 1 lemon
salt and pepper
chopped chives and lemon slices to garnish

1. Slightly warm the clear chicken broth.
2. Beat the eggs together with the grated lemon rind and the lemon juice.
3. Add some of the soup and mix well; then blend with remaining soup.
4. Heat very gently until the soup thickens but do not boil.
5. Allow to cool and then refrigerate. Season with salt and pepper.
6. Serve very cold garnished with chopped chives and lemon slices.

BERGEN FISH SOUP
Serves 6–8

In the coastal areas of Europe substantial fish soups are well liked; this recipe comes from Bergen in Norway.

2oz (50gm) parsnips, coarsely chopped
4oz (100gm) carrots, coarsely chopped
1 large onion, coarsely chopped
1 potato, peeled and chopped
1 teaspoon salt
7 whole black peppercorns
1 tablespoon chopped parsley stems
1 bayleaf
4 sticks celery with leaves or celeriac tops
2½lb (1¼ kilo) fish trimmings (heads, bones, etc. washed)
8 pints (approximately 4 litres) water
4oz (100gm) carrots, finely chopped
2oz (50gm) parsnips, finely chopped
1½lb (¾ kilo) boneless halibut, cod or haddock, in one piece
4oz (100gm) leeks (white parts only), finely chopped
2 large egg yolks
salt and freshly ground pepper
3 tablespoons chopped parsley
6 tablespoons soured cream (optional)

1. To prepare fish stock, which is the base of the soup, combine the first 11 ingredients listed in a very large saucepan or soup kettle.
2. Bring to the boil, partially cover the pan, turn the heat low and simmer for 30–40 minutes.
3. Strain the stock through a fine sieve into a large bowl, pressing down hard on the vegetable and fish trimmings with the back of a spoon to extract juices before discarding the vegetables etc.
4. Wash the pan and return the strained stock to it.
5. Reduce the stock to about 3 pints (approximately 1½ litres) by boiling it rapidly, uncovered for about 20 minutes.
6. Re-strain through a fine sieve or through a double thickness of butter muslin.
7. Again return the stock to the pan. Add the finely chopped carrots, parsnips and the fish in 1 piece. As soon as the soup reaches the boil, lower the heat and simmer uncovered for about 10 minutes.
8. Add the leeks and simmer for a further 2–3 minutes. Remove from the heat, lift out the fish with a slotted spoon and set aside on a dish.
9. In a small bowl, beat the egg yolks with a wire whisk, then beat in about ¼ pint (125ml) of the hot soup, 1 tablespoon at a time. Pour this back into the soup in a thin stream, beating continuously with a wire whisk.
10. With a fork, separate the fish into flakes and add it to the soup.
11. Season with salt and black pepper and reheat, but do not let the soup boil.
12. Serve in individual bowls and sprinkle with chopped parsley. If liked, garnish each serving with 1 tablespoon of soured cream.

BOUILLABAISSE
Serves 4

The famous southern French fish soup – a meal in itself.

1 large packet frozen cod fillets
1 packet frozen prawns
1¼lb (600gm) fish including sea bream or bass, red mullet, eel, mackerel, haddock or sole, whiting or John Dory
1lb (½ kilo) lobster or crab
12 mussels
6 tablespoons olive oil
1 large carrot, chopped
1 onion, chopped
1 leek (white part only), thinly sliced
1 garlic clove, crushed
2 tomatoes, peeled and quartered
2 pints (approximately 1 litre) water
salt and pepper
1 bayleaf
2–3 teaspoons chopped parsley
pinch powdered saffron
4 slices French bread, toasted

1. Gut, wash and cut fish into pieces.
2. Cut the shellfish into large pieces and discard inedible parts.
3. Scrub mussels thoroughly and discard the beards.
4. Heat 1–2 tablespoons oil in a large heavy saucepan, add the carrot, onion, leek and fry until brown.
5. Add the garlic, tomatoes, water and the fish (except the mussels), then season with salt and pepper.
6. Add the bayleaf, parsley and saffron.
7. Cover the pan and bring the ingredients to the boil.
8. Pour on the remaining olive oil and boil briskly for 10 minutes.
9. Add the mussels and cook for a further 8–10 minutes.
10. Remove the mussel shells. Put a slice of toast into each warmed soup bowl. Pour the soup on to the toast and serve.

TUNA SOUP PROVENÇALE
Serves 4

1 can (7oz or 175gm) tuna
1 tablespoon olive oil
1 medium onion, peeled and chopped
1 small red pepper, de-seeded and chopped
1 medium potato, finely sliced
1 can (8oz or 200gm) tomatoes
1 bayleaf
½ pint (250ml) water

1. Put the oil from the tuna and the olive oil into a pan.
2. Add the onion, pepper and potato. Cook gently for 10 minutes.
3. Add the tomatoes, roughly chopped, and their juice, the bayleaf and the water. Season and bring to the boil. Simmer for 20 minutes.
4. Flake the tuna and add it to the soup.
5. Simmer further 5 minutes and serve either hot or cold.

MALAGUENA SOUP
Serves 4–6

Spain's version of a thick fish soup.

12oz (300gm) sea bass
10oz (250gm) shrimps
1¼lb (500gm) clams
12oz (300gm) hake
1 onion, chopped
4 eggs
½ pint (250ml) cooking oil
juice of 1 lemon
salt and pepper

1. Simmer the prepared fish, shellfish and onion in about 3 pints (approximately 1½ litres) water.
2. Strain when fish is cooked and reserve the liquor.
3. Carefully bone the fish and shell the shrimps and clams. Cut into small pieces and place in a saucepan.
4. Beat together the egg yolks, the oil and lemon juice.
5. When this mixture has thickened, slowly add the hot fish broth, beating all the time.
6. Add to the fish and shellfish in the pan and season to taste. Heat through but do not allow to boil, then serve at once.

PORTUGUESE CHICKEN SOUP
Serves 4

This soup is known as *canja* in Portugal.

4oz (100gm) fat bacon or ham, chopped
1½ pints (approximately ¾ litre) chicken stock
seasoning
4½oz (112gm) long-grain rice
3 tablespoons chopped mint (optional)
little lemon juice (optional)

1. Simmer bacon in chicken stock for 15 minutes.
2. Add seasoning and rice and simmer until the rice is cooked.
3. Serve, adding the chopped mint and a little lemon juice if liked.

TOMATO SOUP SPANISH STYLE
Serves 3–4

1 packet (1 pint or approximately ½ litre) tomato soup
1 pint (approximately ½ litre) water
2 large garlic cloves, crushed
1 large onion, finely chopped
1 cucumber, peeled and diced
freshly ground pepper and salt
1 teaspoon vinegar
crushed ice
diced bread, oven toasted or fried

1. Empty the contents of the soup packet into a saucepan and blend in the water.
2. Add the garlic, onion and most of the cucumber.
3. Bring to the boil, stirring, and simmer for 5 minutes with the pan partially covered.
4. Rub through a sieve, or blend in a liquidizer. Add pepper and salt to taste. Chill.
5. Stir in the vinegar and a little crushed ice, then garnish with the remaining cucumber and the diced bread.

GAZPACHO 1
(Illustrated on page 18)
Serves 4

1lb (½ kilo) tomatoes
1 small onion, sliced
1 small green pepper, sliced
1 garlic clove, crushed
1 tablespoon wine vinegar
1 tablespoon olive oil
1–2 tablespoons lemon juice
salt and pepper

Garnishes:
¼ cucumber
2 slices toast
1 red pepper
1 green pepper
3 tomatoes, skinned and de-seeded
1 Spanish onion

1. Wash the tomatoes, dry and slice roughly.
2. Put in a liquidizer with the onion, pepper, garlic, vinegar and olive oil and blend together.
3. Pour into a basin, add lemon juice and seasoning to taste.
4. Chill very well in the refrigerator before serving in small soup bowls.
5. To prepare the garnishes, dice the cucumber, toast, peppers and tomatoes.
6. Finely chop the onion.
7. Put each into a bowl and hand round with the soup.

GAZPACHO 2
Serves 6

1 garlic clove
1 onion, peeled
1 pepper, de-seeded
½ cucumber
1 can (19½oz or 487gm) tomato juice
6 tablespoons olive oil
4 tablespoons lemon juice
salt
cayenne pepper
2 tomatoes
2 thick slices bread, diced
1oz (25gm) butter

1. In a liquidizer, blend the garlic, half the onion, half the pepper, a quarter of a cucumber and a little tomato juice (or cook for 10 minutes, then sieve them).
2. Add the remaining tomato juice, the olive oil, lemon juice, and salt and cayenne to taste. Stir well, pour into a tureen and chill.
3. Slice the remaining onion and pepper, dice the cucumber and tomatoes and place in separate bowls.
4. Fry the diced bread in the butter, turning frequently until browned. Drain and place in a serving bowl.
5. Serve the chilled soup with a slice of onion or pepper floating on the surface. The diced vegetables and croûtons are served as an accompaniment.

ICED PIMENTO SOUP
Serves 4

1 can pimentos
1 can (14oz or 350gm) tomato juice
2 teaspoons tomato purée
salt and pepper
1 teaspoon caster sugar
2 teaspoons lemon juice
chopped parsley and lemon curls to garnish

1. Drain the pimentos and cut two into very thin slices.
2. Mash the rest with a fork until puréed.
3. Add tomato juice and tomato purée, salt, pepper, sugar and lemon juice.
4. Heat gently just to boiling point.
5. Add the sliced pimentos, cool, then refrigerate.
6. Serve garnished with chopped parsley and curls of lemon peel.

TZATZIKI
Serves 4

A chilled soup from Greece.

2 cartons natural yogurt
½ pint (250ml) milk
1 garlic clove, crushed
1 small cucumber, grated
1 tablespoon olive oil
1 tablespoon vinegar
seasoning

1. Beat yogurt.
2. Add the remaining ingredients.
3. Chill well before serving.

SPANISH SPINACH SOUP
Serves 6–8

2 ripe avocados
1 large packet frozen spinach, cooked and drained
1½ pints (approximately ¾ litre) chicken stock
½ pint (250ml) double cream
½ teaspoon salt
½ teaspoon onion salt
pepper
¼ teaspoon grated lemon peel
3 tablespoons lemon juice
lemon slices and hard-boiled egg yolks to garnish

1. Purée the avocado flesh with the spinach.
2. Blend with remaining ingredients. Cover and chill thoroughly.
3. Serve garnished with lemon slices and sieved hard-boiled egg yolks.

COLD RASPBERRY SOUP
(Illustrated on page 18)
Serves 4

A French idea using fruit to make a cool summer soup.

1lb (¼ kilo) fresh raspberries
2 tablespoons honey
5 tablespoons red wine
1 small carton soured cream

1. Rub the raspberries through a fine sieve – this should give ½ pint (250ml) purée.
2. Put the honey, together with 2 tablespoons wine in a small saucepan and heat gently until the honey has dissolved.
3. Leave for a few minutes to cool and then stir into the raspberry purée. Stir in half the soured cream.
4. Add the rest of the wine and ⅓ pint (170ml) cold water. Stir again.
5. Chill for several hours.
6. Serve in bowls with small spoonfuls of soured cream floating on top. Serve with extra soured cream.

FRENCH MUSTARD, HERB AND GARLIC LOAF
Serves 4

A delicious accompaniment to both soups and salads.

3oz (75gm) butter
2–3 garlic cloves
2 teaspoons French mustard
½ teaspoon mixed herbs
salt and black pepper
1 French loaf

1. Preheat oven to moderate to moderately hot, 400 deg F or gas 6 (200 deg C).
2. Soften the butter.
3. Crush or finely chop the garlic and beat together with the butter, mustard and herbs.
4. Season to taste with salt and black pepper.
5. Cut the loaf diagonally into slices, thick or thin, without cutting all the way through.
6. Spread the butter between the slices and scrape a little over the top of the loaf.
7. Wrap the loaf in foil and heat for 15–20 minutes in the centre of the oven, opening the foil for the last 5 minutes. Serve hot.

FRENCH RICE SALAD
Serves 4

6oz (150gm) long-grain rice
¾ pint (375ml) water
¾ teaspoon salt
6oz (150gm) blue cheese, crumbled
¼ pint (125ml) soured cream
1 tablespoon lemon juice
½ celery head, finely chopped
½ cucumber, cubed
1 bunch radishes, sliced
1 bunch chives, chopped
salt and pepper
4 tomatoes, sliced

1. Put the rice, water and salt into saucepan.
2. Bring to the boil and stir once.
3. Lower heat to simmer. Cover and cook for 15 minutes, or until rice is tender and liquid absorbed.
4. Mix cheese, soured cream and lemon juice together.
5. Mix together cooled, cooked rice, celery, cucumber, radishes and chives.
6. Season with salt and pepper Add tomato slices.
7. Chill the salad. Spoon over the cheese mixture before serving.

SPANISH SALAD
Serves 4

3oz (75gm) long-grain rice
1 carrot, grated
few cooked peas
1 small green pepper, de-seeded and diced
2–3 tomatoes, sliced
few black olives, sliced
French dressing (see Basic recipes, page 100)

1. Cook the rice in salted water until tender; drain and cool.
2. Add the vegetables and olives, making sure that all ingredients are blended together and toss in French dressing.
3. Chill thoroughly before serving.

ITALIAN HAM AND PASTA SALAD
Serves 4

4oz (100gm) medium pasta shells
8oz (200gm) cooked ham, diced
6oz (150gm) Bel Paese cheese, diced
2–3 stalks celery, chopped
3–4 spring onions, chopped
2 teaspoons made mustard
¼ pint (125ml) mayonnaise
lettuce, hard-boiled egg slices and tomato slices to garnish

1. Cook the pasta shells in plenty of boiling salted water for 11 minutes, drain well and leave to get cold.
2. Put the ham, cheese, celery and onions in a bowl and mix well.
3. Add the cold pasta and lightly mix with other ingredients.
4. Stir the mustard into the mayonnaise, pour over pasta mixture and toss all lightly together.
5. Serve on lettuce and garnish with hard-boiled egg and tomato slices.

PASTA SLAW
Serves 4

3oz (75gm) spaghetti rings
3oz (75gm) white cabbage, finely shredded
1oz (25gm) green pepper, diced
1oz (25gm) carrot, grated
4 tablespoons mayonnaise
1 tablespoon soured cream
1 tablespoon vinegar
½oz (12gm) sugar

1. Cook the spaghetti rings in plenty of salted boiling water for 10–12 minutes, until just tender. Drain. Refresh with cold water and drain again.
2. Place the prepared vegetables in a bowl.
3. Stir in the cooked pasta.
4. Mix the mayonnaise, soured cream, vinegar and sugar together, then pour over the salad. Toss.
5. Allow to stand in a cool place for 1 hour before serving.

ITALIAN SALAD
Serves 4

5oz (125gm) pasta spirals
1 can (5oz or 125gm) salata
1 can (5oz or 125gm) crushed pineapple
1oz (25gm) currants
salt and pepper
2 tablespoons French dressing (see Basic recipes, page 100)

1. Cook the pasta in boiling salted water for 8 minutes, drain and refresh with cold water. Drain again.
2. Place pasta in a bowl and add remaining ingredients.
3. Mix well and serve.

MACARONI SALAD
Serves 4

4oz (100gm) macaroni
1½ tablespoons lemon juice
1 tablespoon olive oil
2 tablespoons vinegar
2 tablespoons chopped chives
or 1 teaspoon grated onion
3–4 sticks celery with leaves
3 tablespoons chopped parsley
2 tablespoons chopped canned
pimento
12 stuffed olives, chopped
3 tablespoons soured cream
lettuce and tomato slices to
garnish

1. Cook macaroni in plenty of
boiling salted water until just
tender.
2. Mix the lemon juice, oil and
vinegar well together.
3. When the macaroni is cooked,
drain it well and while still hot,
toss in the dressing and set aside
to cool.
4. Mix remaining ingredients,
season with salt and freshly
ground pepper.
5. When ready to serve, mix with
macaroni and arrange on lettuce
and garnish with tomato slices.

PRAGUE EGG SALAD
Serves 6

10oz (250gm) ham, chopped
7oz (175gm) cooked potatoes,
sliced
2–3 gherkins, sliced
3oz (75gm) root vegetables,
cut in strips
3oz (75gm) cooked peas
6 tablespoons mayonnaise
salt and pepper
1 tablespoon vinegar
6 hard-boiled eggs
6 tablespoons bottled tartare
sauce

1. Mix the ham, potatoes,
gherkins, root vegetables and
peas together.
2. Mix the mayonnaise with salt,
pepper and vinegar.
3. Toss the ham etc. in a bowl
with the mayonnaise mixture.
4. Arrange the hard-boiled egg
slices on top and spoon over
tartare sauce.

SALAD MORAVIAN STYLE
Serves 4–6

3½oz (87gm) smoked meat
3½oz (87gm) roast lean pork
3½oz (87gm) gherkins
1 hard-boiled egg
1 apple
juice of 1 lemon
1 small lettuce
fresh or dried dill
¼ pint (125ml) double cream,
lightly whipped
salt and freshly ground pepper

1. Cut the smoked meat, roast
pork, gherkins and hard-boiled
egg into small cubes.
2. Add the apple, cut in strips,
and sprinkle with the lemon
juice.
4. Add finely shredded lettuce,
chopped dill and whipped cream.
5. Mix well together, season to
taste.
6. Serve slightly chilled.

DANISH SUMMER SALAD
Serves 4–6

1 small chicken
1 onion, sliced
2 carrots
salt
2 hard-boiled eggs
¼ pint (125ml) olive oil
4 tablespoons lemon juice or
vinegar
chopped fresh or dried mint
salt and pepper
½ green pepper, sliced
3 tomatoes, sliced
2oz (50gm) raw cauliflower
sprigs
1 small lettuce, finely shredded

1. Boil or steam the chicken with
the onion, carrots and salt until
tender.
2. Remove meat from bone and
cut in fine strips.
3. Slice the eggs.
4. Mix the olive oil, lemon juice
or vinegar, mint and seasoning
for the dressing and leave for 1
hour.
5. Mix chicken pieces and eggs
with the pepper, tomatoes,
cauliflower and lettuce in a large
bowl and carefully add the
dressing.

HUSSARS' SALAD
Serves 6

8oz (200gm) cooked meat
8oz (200gm) cooked potatoes
1 cooking apple
1 small beetroot, cooked
few gherkins
2 hard-boiled eggs
8 silverskin onions
2 tablespoons oil
2 tablespoons vinegar
salt and pepper
mustard
pinch of nutmeg
1 lettuce
mayonnaise
hard-boiled egg slices and
paprika pepper to garnish

1. Cube meat, potatoes, apple,
beetroot and gherkins.
2. Chop eggs and halve onions.
3. Make dressing with the oil,
vinegar, salt, pepper, mustard and
nutmeg.
4. Toss ingredients in dressing.
5. Arrange lettuce on a dish and
pile the salad mixture on top.
6. Spoon over mayonnaise and
garnish with hard-boiled egg
slices and paprika pepper.

RADISH SALAD
Serves 4

A piquant salad, from Holland,
to serve as a side dish and one
which shows the Continental love
of soured cream in salads.

1 bunch radishes
1 carton (5oz or 125gm) soured
cream
¼ pint (125ml) yogurt
1 egg yolk
½ garlic clove, finely chopped
(optional)
salt and pepper

1. Grate the radishes finely.
2. Mix the remaining ingredients
together and stir in the radishes.
3. Serve slightly chilled.

HUNGARIAN DRESSING
Serves 4–6

A Hungarian yogurt dressing ideal on a green or tomato salad.

2oz (50gm) streaky bacon rashers
1 carton (5oz or 125gm) natural yogurt
1 level teaspoon grated onion
¼ teaspoon Tabasco sauce

1. Remove rind from bacon and grill rashers until very crisp.
2. Drain on kitchen paper.
3. Mix yogurt, onion and Tabasco sauce together.
4. Just before serving crumble in bacon.
5. Serve on a green or tomato salad.

CUCUMBER AND YOGURT SALAD
(Illustrated on page 18)
Serves 4–5

A popular side salad in the Eastern Mediterranean countries.

1 cucumber, peeled and diced
3 garlic cloves, chopped
2 cartons (5oz or 125gm) natural yogurt (soured cream can be substituted)
2–3 tablespoons finely chopped mint
salt and freshly ground pepper

1. Place the cucumber in a colander, sprinkle liberally with salt and set aside, under a heavy weight, for 30 minutes.
2. Mix together the garlic, yogurt, mint, salt and pepper.
3. Rinse the cucumber under cold running water.
4. Drain well and mix with the yogurt mixture.
5. Serve slightly chilled as an accompaniment to lamb chops.

CUCUMBER SALAD
Serves 4

A refreshing side salad from Denmark.

1 cucumber
6 tablespoons white vinegar
6 tablespoons water
6 tablespoons sugar
salt and pepper

1. Wash and peel the cucumber. Slice thinly, sprinkle lightly with salt and let stand for 15 minutes.
2. Pour off all juice or moisture.
3. Mix the remaining ingredients together, add salt and pepper to taste, and pour over cucumber.
4. Allow to stand for 1 hour before serving.

POLISH SALAD
Serves 4

1lb (½ kilo) frozen peas
10 prunes, soaked
10 black olives
6 plums, pickled in vinegar
1 apple
juice of 1 lemon
1 stick celery
3 hard-boiled eggs
½ pint (250ml) mayonnaise
1 teaspoon mustard
2 garlic cloves
salt and sugar to taste
chopped parsley to garnish

1. Cook the peas in boiling salted water, with a little sugar added, until they become soft – about 10 minutes.
2. Drain and cool.
3. Drain the prunes then stone them and cut into strips. Cut olives and pickled plums into strips.
4. Grate the apple, sprinkle with lemon juice.
6. Chop the celery and slice the eggs.
7. Mix mayonnaise with mustard and finely chopped garlic.
8. Combine and mix all ingredients with the mayonnaise. Season with salt and sugar.
9. Serve sprinkled with chopped parsley.

SWISS MUSHROOM SALAD
Serves 6

6–8oz (150–200gm) Emmental cheese
6 hard-boiled eggs
1 heaped teaspoon dry mustard
1 teaspoon grated horseradish
1 carton (5oz or 125gm) soured cream
salt and pepper
4oz (100gm) button mushrooms
1 lettuce or head chicory
mushroom slices to garnish

1. Cut the cheese into 1-inch strips.
2. Slice the hard-boiled eggs, keep a few rings for garnish, and coarsely chop the rest.
3. Blend the mustard and horseradish with soured cream and season with salt and pepper.
4. Toss the cheese, mushrooms and eggs in the soured cream sauce.
5. Serve on lettuce or chicory. Garnish with hard-boiled egg and mushroom slices.

RUMANIAN AUBERGINE SALAD
Serves 4

2 medium aubergines
½ pint (125ml) olive oil
1 small onion
salt and pepper
red pepper slices to garnish

1. Grill the aubergines whole until the skins are charred almost black.
2. Rinse in cold water and skin them carefully.
3. Mash the pulp with a wooden spoon, then add the olive oil, drop by drop, stirring vigorously, until the mixture is a smooth thick purée.
4. Add the finely chopped onion, salt and pepper.
5. Garnish with thin slices of red pepper and serve cold.

POTATO SALAD
(Illustrated on page 35)
Serves 6–8

In Germany *kartoffel salat* is served with hot or cold dishes.

1½–2lb (¾–1 kilo) new potatoes
1 teaspoon finely chopped parsley
1 teaspoon finely chopped onion
1 teaspoon finely chopped chives
salt and pepper
2 tablespoons olive oil
1 tablespoon wine vinegar
cucumber slices to garnish

1. Boil the potatoes in their skins.
2. When cooked, peel the potatoes and slice while still hot.
3. Put into a salad bowl in layers, and sprinkle parsley, onion, chives and seasoning between each layer.
4. Mix the oil and vinegar and pour over the salad.
5. Garnish with cucumber slices and serve chilled.

MEDITERRANEAN SALAD
(Illustrated on page 35)
Serves 4

1 packet frozen haricots verts
1 packet frozen sweetcorn
1 can pimentos, chopped
4 black olives, chopped (optional)
1 small onion, finely chopped
3 tablespoons oil
2 tablespoons vinegar
black pepper
1 teaspoon salt
2 teaspoons sugar

1. Cook the haricots verts in boiling salted water for 5 minutes.
2. Drain and run cold water over them for 1 minute.
3. Cook the sweetcorn according to the packet instructions; drain and cool.
4. Mix with pimentos, beans, olives and onion.
5. To make the dressing put the remaining ingredients into a screwtop jar and shake vigorously until thickened.
6. Blend with the vegetables and chill for several hours before serving.

DANISH HERRING AND MUSHROOM SALAD
Serves 4

4oz (100gm) button mushrooms
2 tablespoons vinegar
4 tablespoons salad oil
½ teaspoon salt
½ teaspoon sugar
½ teaspoon dry mustard
pepper
4 bismarck (or luncheon) herrings
onion rings pickled with herrings and parsley sprigs to garnish

1. Wash, but do not peel, mushrooms and cut them into thin slices.
2. Blend together the vinegar, oil, salt, sugar, mustard and pepper and lightly mix with mushrooms.
3. Place herrings, well apart, on a serving dish and pile dressed mushrooms between them.
4. Garnish with onion rings and parsley sprigs.

HOLSTEIN HERRING
Serves 4

4 herrings
salt and pepper
½ pint (250ml) malt vinegar and water mixed
1 tablespoon pickling spice
4 bayleaves
2 small onions, sliced
½ cucumber
1 carton soured cream
parsley to garnish

1. Preheat oven to cool, 275 deg F or gas 1 (140 deg C).
2. Scale, clean and bone herrings.
3. Season well with salt and pepper and roll up, skin outwards, beginning at the tail.
4. Place rolls neatly and fairly closely together in an ovenproof dish.
5. Cover with vinegar and water and scatter with pickling spice, crushed bayleaves and onion rings.
6. Cover with foil or lid and bake in the centre of the oven for about 1½ hours.
7. Cool, then drain off liquid and reserve onion rings for garnish.
8. Cut four slices of cucumber for garnish.
9. Peel and dice the remainder of

the cucumber and mix with cream.
10. Arrange herrings on a dish and spoon soured cream mixture in centre. Garnish with onion rings, cucumber slices and parsley.

SWEDISH ROE SALAD
Serves 4

8oz (200gm) soft herring roes
1½oz (37gm) flour seasoned with salt and pepper
1½oz (37gm) butter for frying
3 tablespoons French dressing (see Basic recipes, page 100)
1 apple, sliced
2 sticks celery, diced
4oz (100gm) white cabbage, shredded
¼ cucumber, peeled and diced
chopped parsley to garnish

1. Coat roes in seasoned flour and fry lightly in butter.
2. Drain on kitchen paper. Cool.
3. Marinate in French dressing for 1 hour.
4. Mix with apple and vegetables just before serving and garnish with coarsely chopped parsley.

ROTTERDAM CUCUMBER SALAD
Serves 4

2 medium cucumbers
6 teaspoons salad oil
6 tablespoons vinegar
juice of 2 lemons
salt and pepper
pinch of sugar and paprika pepper
8oz (200gm) cheese, grated

1. Wash, dry and slice cucumbers.
2. Pour oil into a basin.
3. Stir in vinegar, lemon juice, salt, pepper, sugar and paprika pepper.
4. Stir until thoroughly blended.
5. Mix with grated cheese.
6. Arrange cucumber slices in a salad bowl.
7. Spoon dressing in the centre.

Meat, poultry and game

Recipes are given here for using all types of meat and poultry, including the cheaper cuts, such as pie veal, which can be made into really delicious main course dishes.

Meat dishes in Europe tend to be much more complex and subtle than our roast beef or lamb joints, which need no more than a simple gravy and vegetables to go with them.

Europeans have learnt to flavour and sauce their meats into delicious dishes. Pot roasting is widespread; soured cream and wine are used to make sauces. Pasta, rice and vegetables make meats go further. Lamb, a popular meat in eastern countries, is served in many ways – as kebabs and in Greek lamb stews. Veal is a much more important meat than in Britain and there are many delightful ways of using offal. Steaks aren't just grilled, but presented in a variety of unusual ways, including spiced and raw as in steak tartare.

POLISH BEEF WITH TOMATOES
Serves 4

1lb ($\frac{1}{2}$ kilo) beef topside or silverside
2 tablespoons olive oil
juice of $\frac{1}{2}$ lemon
2 onions
1 carrot
5oz (125gm) tomatoes, peeled
$\frac{1}{2}$oz (12gm) butter
pinch of basil
1 bayleaf
3–4 grains allspice
salt and pepper
$\frac{1}{2}$ glass dry white wine
$\frac{1}{4}$ glass Madeira

1. Brown the meat in the oil, sprinkle with lemon juice and add finely chopped onions, carrot and sliced tomatoes.
2. Add butter and seasonings, and simmer, with the lid on, sprinkling the meat now and again with the wine mixed with the Madeira, until the meat is tender.
3. Remove meat from pan and slice. Keep warm.
4. Sieve the sauce, adjust seasoning and reheat.
5. Serve the meat with the sauce poured over.

BOEUF BOURGUIGNON
Serves 4

1$\frac{1}{2}$lb ($\frac{3}{4}$ kilo) stewing beef, cubed
$\frac{1}{2}$oz (12gm) flour, seasoned with salt and pepper
1oz (25gm) dripping
2 streaky bacon rashers, chopped
12 small onions
2oz (50gm) mushrooms, peeled and sliced
pinch of sugar
$\frac{1}{4}$ pint (125ml) red wine
$\frac{1}{2}$ pint (250ml) stock
seasoning
bouquet garni
chopped parsley to garnish

1. Coat beef cubes in seasoned flour.
2. Melt dripping, add meat and brown well on all sides.
3. Remove meat and add bacon, onions, mushrooms and sugar. Brown gently.
4. Remove mushrooms and onions, return meat, heat the wine and add to pan together with stock to cover. Add seasoning and bouquet garni.
5. Cover and simmer for 1 hour.
6. Add onions and mushrooms, and continue cooking for another hour.
7. Garnish with chopped parsley and serve with creamed potatoes.

Potato salad (see page 33)   Mediterranean salad (see page 33)

Spanish pot roast (see page 38)   Boeuf Stroganoff (see page 42)

Neapolitan lamb chops (see page 47)   Veal cacciatora (see page 46)

Stuffed calf's liver à Transmontana (see page 50)   Chicken chasseur marengo (see page 52)

FONDUE BOURGUIGNONNE
Serves 4–6

A French meat fondue with accompanying sauces.

oil for frying
1½lb (¾ kilo) fillet or rump steak, cut in cubes

1. Put enough cooking oil into fondue pot to fill it half full. Heat oil on the cooker until it reaches 375 deg F (190 deg C). Test with a thermometer, or a cube of bread – it should brown in less than 1 minute.
2. Transfer pot immediately to the stand, and keep oil hot by adjusting the flame underneath.
3. Each person spears a cube of meat on to a fork, and places it in the hot oil. The meat takes only a few moments to cook, the exact time depending on individual preference.
4. The meat is then dipped in a sauce and transferred to another fork for eating. Do not attempt to eat direct from the fondue forks as they can burn the mouth. Serve a selection or all of the following sauces with your beef fondue.

MUSHROOM SOURED CREAM SAUCE

1oz (25gm) butter
1 onion, finely chopped
4oz (100gm) mushrooms, finely chopped
1 tablespoon chopped parsley
2 cartons (5oz or 125gm) soured cream
salt and pepper
¼ teaspoon Tabasco sauce

1. Melt butter in pan. Add onion and mushrooms and cook gently until tender but not brown. Drain well and cool.
2. Add onion, mushrooms and parsley to soured cream.
3. Stir in seasoning and Tabasco sauce. Mix all together. If sauce is too thick, add a little milk.

SAVOURY SAUCE

¼ pint (125ml) mayonnaise
3–4 tablespoons tomato sauce
½ teaspoon Tabasco sauce
1 teaspoon vinegar
2 tablespoons finely chopped onion
2 gherkins, finely chopped
salt and sugar to taste

1. Mix the mayonnaise with the tomato sauce, Tabasco sauce and vinegar.
2. Stir in the chopped onion and gherkins. Add salt and sugar.

BARBECUE SAUCE

1 medium onion, chopped
4 tablespoons olive oil
5 tablespoons tomato ketchup
½ pint (250ml) water
2oz (50gm) demerara sugar
¼ teaspoon Worcestershire sauce
1 teaspoon salt
juice of ½ lemon
1 tablespoon wine vinegar
1 teaspoon Tabasco sauce

1. Fry onion in 1 tablespoon oil until transparent.
2. Mix together remaining ingredients and add to onion.
3. Cook over low heat for 20 minutes.

DIABLE SAUCE

1 tablespoon chopped onion
1oz (25gm) butter
1½ level tablespoons flour
½ pint (250ml) stock
1 tablespoon vinegar
½ bayleaf
6–8 peppercorns, crushed
8–10 drops Tabasco sauce
½ teaspoon English mustard

1. Cook the onion in butter until soft and transparent.
2. Add the flour and cook for a few minutes.
3. Add stock and vinegar and stir until boiling.
4. Add bayleaf and peppercorns and simmer for 10 minutes.
5. Strain, then add Tabasco sauce and mustard. Serve cold.

BEEF BORDELAISE
Serves 6

1½lb (¾ kilo) braising steak
1 garlic clove
1 rounded teaspoon salt
½ level teaspoon pepper
1 bayleaf
2 cloves
1 level teaspoon dried thyme
¼ pint (125ml) red wine
6 small onions
6 mushrooms
2 medium carrots
3 tablespoons oil
¾ pint (250ml) beef stock
2 parsley sprigs
8oz (200gm) French beans, sliced and cooked

1. Trim the beef and cut into cubes.
2. Peel and crush garlic and place in bowl with salt, pepper, bayleaf, cloves, thyme and wine.
3. Add meat and leave overnight in a cool place.
4. Next day, drain meat, reserving marinade.
5. Peel onions and keep whole.
6. Wash and dry mushrooms – keep whole if small, otherwise slice.
7. Peel carrots and cut in rings.
8. Heat oil in saucepan, add meat and fry for a few minutes.
7. Add reserved marinade, stock and parsley.
10. Bring to boil and simmer for 15 minutes.
11. Reduce heat, cover and simmer very slowly for 1¼ hours.
13. Add onions, mushrooms and carrots and continue to simmer for a further 45 minutes, or until meat is tender.
13. Just before serving, adjust seasoning, stir in cooked beans and heat through.

SPANISH POT ROAST

(Illustrated on page 35)
Serves 4

2 tablespoons oil
2lb (1 kilo) topside, or similar
joint suitable for pot roasting,
rolled and tied
1 large onion, sliced
1 green pepper, cut in rings
3 sticks celery, chopped
1 can (8oz or 200gm) tomatoes
2 teaspoons tomato purée
generous pinch of brown sugar
1 dessertspoon dry mustard
⅓ pint (170ml) red wine

1. Heat oil in heavy casserole –
preferably one into which the
meat just fits.
2. Brown meat on all sides in the
hot oil.
3. Remove meat and fry onion
until soft.
4. Replace the meat, add the
pepper, celery and tomatoes.
5. Mix the tomato purée with a
little water and the brown sugar
and add to casserole.
6. Sprinkle on the mustard and
pour on the wine.
7. Cover tightly and simmer
gently for about 3 hours until
meat is tender.

POT-AU-FEU

Serves 6

A classic French way of stewing
beef; the stock becomes the first
course soup.

2½lb (1¼ kilo) beef topside
8 leeks, washed and shredded
3 large carrots, peeled and
sliced
1 large onion, peeled and stuck
with 4 cloves
1lb (½ kilo) turnips, peeled and
cut
2 bayleaves
sprig of thyme and parsley
1 stick celery, diced
2 teaspoons salt
6 black peppercorns
2lb (1 kilo) potatoes, peeled

1. Trim excess fat from the beef
and place in a large saucepan
with all the prepared vegetables
(except the potatoes), seasoning
and herbs.
2. Add enough water to cover and
simmer gently for 2½ hours.
3. Add the potatoes and simmer
for a further 20 minutes.
4. Adjust the seasoning if
necessary and strain the stock to
serve as a first course.
5. Slice the meat and serve on a
large flat dish, surrounded by the
vegetables. Serve with gherkins,
pickles and mustard, salted butter
and bread.

HUNGARIAN GOULASH

Serves 4

1lb (½ kilo) rump or buttock
steak
½oz (12gm) dripping, if
necessary
1lb (½ kilo) onions, thinly sliced
1–2 garlic cloves, chopped
1 level tablespoon paprika
pepper
salt and pepper
½ level teaspoon caraway seeds
½oz (12gm) flour
1 tablespoon tomato purée
¾ pint (375ml) beef stock
4 tablespoons yogurt or soured
cream

1. Wipe and trim the meat. Chop
up the fat into very small pieces.
2. Put into a heavy stewpan
together with a little dripping if
necessary. Heat gently until the
fat begins to melt.
3. Add the meat, cut in small
pieces, and the onions and garlic.
Sauté until the meat is browned.
4. Stir in the paprika pepper,
seasoning and caraway seeds.
Sauté for 2–3 minutes.
5. Cover closely and cook over a
very low heat for 40–50 minutes,
stirring once or twice.
6. Add the flour, tomato purée
and beef stock. Cover and simmer
gently for another hour, then
taste, add seasoning if necessary.
7. Just before serving, stir in
yogurt or soured cream.

BEEF PROVENÇALE
Serves 4

1½ tablespoons olive oil
½ carrot, sliced
½ onion, sliced
½ glass red or white wine
½ tablespoon wine vinegar
bouquet garni or 1 teaspoon
mixed herbs
1lb (½ kilo) braising steak
(in largish pieces)
1oz (25gm) fat
1lb (½ kilo) potatoes, peeled and
sliced
8oz (200gm) carrots, sliced
1 garlic clove, peeled and
crushed
1oz (25gm) black olives, stoned
½ pint (250ml) beef stock or
water
8oz (200gm) tomatoes, skinned
and sliced
salt and pepper
1 teaspoon sugar

1. Mix the first six ingredients
together for the marinade. Bring
to the boil and simmer for 15
minutes. Cool then pour over the
meat in a china bowl. Leave in
the refrigerator overnight.
2. Preheat oven to very moderate,
325 deg F or gas 3 (170 deg C).
3. Strain and reserve marinade;
brown meat quickly in hot fat and
place in deep ovenproof casserole.
4. Add prepared potatoes, carrots,
garlic, olives and stock and
marinade. Cover and cook in the
centre of the oven for 1½ hours.
5. Add tomatoes and cook for a
further 30 minutes.
6. Before serving add salt, pepper
and sugar if necessary.

FLEMISH BEEF
Serves 4

3 tablespoons oil
2 green peppers, seeded and
chopped
2 medium onions, peeled and
chopped
1 garlic clove, peeled and
chopped
2 sticks celery, chopped
1 large carrot, chopped
1½lb (¾ kilo) braising steak, cut
in 1-inch cubes
1oz (25gm) flour
½ pint (250ml) light ale
1 bayleaf
½ level teaspoon dried
marjoram
freshly ground black pepper
salt
1 tablespoon tomato purée
3 tablespoons double cream

1. Preheat oven to moderate, 350
deg F or gas 4 (180 deg C).
2. Heat the oil in a fireproof
casserole and sauté the pepper,
onions, garlic, celery and carrot
until beginning to brown.
3. Toss the steak in the flour and
sauté with the vegetables until
browned.
4. Add the remaining ingredients,
except the cream, cover and cook
in the centre of the oven for 1½–2
hours.
5. Stir in the cream and serve
immediately.

DUTCH HUNTERS' STEW
Serves 4

This dish is known as *jachtschotel*
in Holland.

8oz (200gm) onions
2oz (50gm) butter
8oz (200gm) cooked beef,
finely chopped
½ pint (250ml) stock
pepper, salt and nutmeg
1lb (½ kilo) mashed potatoes
8oz (200gm) apples, peeled and
chopped
1 tablespoon breadcrumbs

1. Preheat oven to moderate to
moderately hot, 375 deg F or gas 5
(190 deg C).
2. Fry onions in 1½oz (37gm) of
the butter until golden brown.
3. Add meat, stock and seasoning,
blend together.
4. Butter an ovenproof dish and
place meat mixture, potatoes and
apples in layers, finishing with a
layer of potatoes.
5. Dot with remaining butter,
sprinkle with breadcrumbs and
cook in the centre of the oven for
20 minutes.

DUTCH STEWED STEAK
Serves 4

In Holland this is called *hachee*.

1½lb (¾ kilo) cold, cooked beef
12oz (300gm) onions
1oz (25gm) dripping
1oz (25gm) flour
1 pint (approximately ½ litre)
stock
2 bayleaves
4 peppercorns
1 tablespoon Worcestershire
sauce
1 tablespoon vinegar
salt and pepper

1. Cube meat and slice onions.
2. Brown onions in the dripping.
Blend in the flour and cook for a
few moments and slowly pour in
the stock, stirring.
3. Bring to the boil, add meat,
bayleaves, peppercorns,
Worcestershire sauce, vinegar,
salt and pepper.
4. Simmer for 1 hour, adjust
seasoning and serve with root
vegetables or cabbage.

DUTCH BOILED BEEF AND VEGETABLES
Serves 4

A popular dish from Holland where it is known as *hutspot*.

1lb (½ kilo) lean beef brisket or silverside
1 pint (approximately ½ litre) water
1½lb (¾ kilo) carrots
2lb (1 kilo) potatoes
12oz (300gm) onions
1 marrow bone
salt and pepper

1. Place meat in a pan with water; bring to the boil and simmer for 1½ hours.
2. Cube carrots and potatoes; slice onions.
3. Add carrots and cook for a further hour, then add the marrow bone, potatoes and onions and simmer until vegetables are tender.
4. Remove the meat, discard the marrow bone and strain off most of the liquid, and mash the vegetables together with remaining liquid and seasoning.
5. Serve the meat on mashed vegetables.

NORWEGIAN HASH
Serves 4

In Norway this is called *pytt i panna*.

2 onions, chopped
2–3oz (50–75gm) butter or margarine
about 2lb (1 kilo) cooked beef, sausage or ham, diced
8 potatoes, boiled and diced
salt and pepper
chopped parsley to garnish

1. Fry the onions in some of the fat until golden brown.
2. Brown the meat and potatoes in the remaining fat. Season.
3. Stir in the onion and adjust seasoning. Sprinkle chopped parsley on top.
4. Serve with fried eggs or raw egg yolks, a green salad and pickled beetroot or salted cucumber.

TOURNEDOS ROSSINI
Serves 4

A party de luxe steak dish.

4 tournedos (round fillet) steaks
freshly ground black pepper
2oz (50gm) butter
2 tablespoons olive oil
4 bread rounds
lemon juice
salt
4 slices pâté de foie gras
12 truffle slices
Madeira sauce (thicken and season beef stock and add a little Madeira wine)

1. Season the tournedos with some black pepper and sauté in butter and olive oil until well browned, about 2–3 minutes on each side.
2. Remove from the pan and keep warm.
3. Sauté the bread in butter.
4. Sprinkle lightly with lemon juice and place a slice of pâté on each bread round and top with a tournedos.
6. Garnish with truffles and pour Madeira sauce around the tournedos.

SWEDISH BEEFSTEAK WITH ONIONS
Serves 4

2lb (1 kilo) sirloin steak
2oz (50gm) butter or margarine
4 onions, sliced
1 teaspoon salt
¼ teaspoon pepper
¼ pint (125ml) boiling water

1. Cut steak into four portions and flatten meat lightly.
2. Melt 2 tablespoons of the fat in a pan.
3. Add onions and fry until softened and brown. Remove onions and keep warm.
4. Add remaining fat to pan, heat.
5. Sprinkle meat with salt and pepper and fry 3–4 minutes each side – longer if desired.
6. Remove meat to a serving dish and keep warm. Pour boiling water into pan and stir to dissolve brown particles; pour over meat.
7. Serve the steaks garnished with the onions.

SWEDISH SAILORS' STEW
Serves 4

A hearty dish for cold days.

1½lb (¾ kilo) chuck steak
5–6 medium potatoes
2oz (50gm) butter or margarine
12oz (300gm) onions, sliced
2 teaspoons salt
pepper
generous ½ pint (250ml) water
generous ½ pint (250ml) beer
chopped parsley to garnish

1. Preheat oven to moderate to moderately hot, 375 deg F or gas 5 (190 deg C).
2. Cut meat into slices and flatten a little.
3. Peel potatoes and cut into slices.
4. Heat fat in pan, add meat and brown quickly on both sides; sprinkle with 1 teaspoon of the the salt; remove from pan.
5. Cook onions in the same pan until brown and then remove.
6. Add water to pan and boil for a few minutes.
7. Place meat, onions and potatoes in alternate layers in a casserole, sprinkling each layer with salt and pepper.
8. Add pan liquid and beer.
9. Cover and cook in centre of the oven for 1–1¼ hours or until meat is tender.
10. Sprinkle with parsley before serving.

PORTUGUESE STEAK AND ONION
Serves 4

2 large onions, sliced
4 tomatoes, peeled and chopped
2 garlic cloves, crushed
salt and pepper
2½oz (62gm) butter
1 tablespoon white vinegar
4 sirloin or rump steaks
parsley to garnish

1. Fry the onions, tomatoes, garlic, salt and pepper in the butter.
2. When the onion is browned add the vinegar and simmer until well blended. Adjust seasoning.
3. Grill the steaks according to taste, then place on a hot serving dish.
4. Spoon the tomato mixture over; garnish with parsley and serve with boiled or fried potatoes.

ITALIAN STEAK WITH TOMATOES AND GARLIC
Serves 4

2 tablespoons olive oil
4 fillet or porterhouse steaks
3 garlic cloves, peeled and chopped
4 tomatoes, peeled and chopped
¼ teaspoon dried oregano
salt and pepper
chopped parsley to garnish

1. Heat the oil and fry the steaks for 1 minute on each side to brown and seal.
2. Remove from the pan and keep hot.
3. Add the garlic and fry until lightly browned.
4. Add the tomatoes and oregano and cook slowly for 5–6 minutes. Season to taste.
5. Replace the steaks and cook for a further 4–5 minutes.
6. Serve garnished with chopped parsley.

BEEF STEAK TARTARE
Serves 4

A raw steak dish with a Russian name that is very popular in Holland.

1lb (½ kilo) fillet steak, finely minced
1 tablespoon chopped gherkins
1 egg yolk
1 tablespoon vegetable oil
1 teaspoon salt
¼ teaspoon freshly milled pepper
1 teaspoon Worcestershire sauce
1 teaspoon paprika pepper
1 tablespoon finely chopped onion
1 tablespoon capers
1 teaspoon made mild mustard
chopped parsley to garnish

1. Mix all the ingredients (except parsley) thoroughly.
2. Serve raw garnished with a little chopped parsley.

BOEUF A LA FICELLE
Serves 4

A dish often served in France at informal dinner parties where a label with the guest's name is tied to each steak, so each person can cook the steak to their own liking.

1 large veal bone, chopped in two, or 1 chicken carcass
3 large carrots, peeled and thickly sliced
1 turnip, quartered
2 leeks
1 onion stuck with 4 cloves
1 stick celery
2 teaspoons salt
6 white peppercorns
bouquet garni
4 fillet steaks, each about 8oz (200gm)

1. Put the veal bone or chicken into a large saucepan with the prepared vegetables, salt, peppercorns, bouquet garni and enough water to cover.
2. Simmer very gently for 2 hours.
3. Strain the stock into a clean saucepan.
4. Tie each piece of steak on a length of thin string and place in the stock.
5. Poach the steaks according to taste and serve with a salad.

BEEF OLIVES
Serves 4

8 streaky bacon rashers
1lb (½ kilo) beef topside, cut into 8 thin slices
1 medium onion, finely chopped
2 small gherkins, finely chopped
1 level teaspoon mixed herbs
2oz (50gm) butter
½ pint (250ml) stock
cornflour

1. Remove the rind from the bacon, stretch the rashers with the back of a knife and put 1 rasher on each slice of topside.
2. Sprinkle with onion, gherkin and herbs.
3. Roll up and tie with string or secure with wooden cocktail sticks.
4. Brown gently all over in butter for about 10 minutes.
5. Add the hot stock, cover and continue cooking for another 10 minutes, until the meat is tender.
6. Thicken the liquid with a little cornflour and cook for a further 4–5 minutes.
7. Remove string or cocktail sticks before serving. Serve with noodles.

BOEUF STROGANOFF
(Illustrated on page 35)
Serves 4–5

A classic Russian dish invented by the chef of the Stroganoff family in Leningrad.

1lb ($\frac{1}{2}$ kilo) rump steak, cut in 1-inch strips
seasoning
generous $\frac{1}{4}$ pint (125ml) red wine
2oz (50gm) butter or margarine
2 medium onions, sliced
4oz (100gm) mushrooms, sliced
salt and black pepper
pinch of nutmeg
1oz (25gm) flour
4 tablespoons tomato purée
$\frac{1}{2}$ pint (250ml) stock or stock and water
$\frac{1}{4}$ pint (125ml) soured cream

1. Two hours before cooking, sprinkle meat with seasoning and most of the red wine, cover and leave to stand.
2. Melt butter or margarine in a large saucepan and fry onions and mushrooms until soft, but not brown.
3. Add the prepared meat and fry gently for 4–5 minutes.
4. Stir in flour and cook for a further 2 minutes.
5. Add tomato purée and stock, and simmer gently for 10–15 minutes.
6. Add remaining wine and the soured cream just before serving. (Do not boil after cream has been added.)

ITALIAN STUFFED MEAT ROLLS
Serves 6

A popular way of serving beef in Italy, known as *braccioli*.

1$\frac{1}{2}$lb ($\frac{3}{4}$ kilo) silverside, cut into 6 slices, or 6 minute steaks
6 back bacon rashers
2 large onions, finely chopped
2oz (50gm) butter
2 tablespoons oil
6oz (150gm) fresh white breadcrumbs
2oz (50gm) cheese, grated
1 level teaspoon marjoram
1oz (25gm) sultanas
1oz (25gm) blanched almonds, chopped
1 teaspoon salt
pepper
3 tablespoons tomato purée
$\frac{1}{2}$ pint (250ml) stock or water

1. Preheat oven to very moderate, 325 deg F or gas 3 (170 deg C).
2. Trim off any excess fat from meat. Lay slices on a board and flatten with a rolling pin until very thin.
3. Fry bacon gently 1 minute each side and place a rasher on each slice of meat.
4. To make stuffing, cook onions gently in butter and half the oil for 3–4 minutes without browning.
5. Add the breadcrumbs, cheese, marjoram, sultanas, almonds and seasoning to half the onions.
6. Divide equally between meat slices and press down. Roll up tightly and secure ends with wooden cocktail sticks.
7. Heat remaining oil in large flameproof casserole. Brown rolls evenly on all sides.
8. Add remaining onion and tomato purée mixed with stock or water, season and bring to the boil.
9. Cover and cook in the centre of the oven for 45 minutes until meat is tender.
10. Serve with spaghetti tossed in butter.

HUNGARIAN MEATBALLS WITH SOURED CREAM
Serves 4

12oz (500gm) minced beef
8oz (200gm) sausagemeat
2 onions, grated
1 egg, beaten
2oz (50gm) breadcrumbs
$\frac{1}{2}$ teaspoon meat extract
$\frac{1}{2}$ level teaspoon mixed dried herbs
salt and pepper
1oz (25gm) lard
1oz (25gm) butter
2 sticks celery, chopped
1 can (14oz or 350gm) tomatoes
1 tablespoon tomato purée
2 level teaspoons cornflour
2 tablespoons water
1 carton (5oz or 125gm) soured cream

1. Combine the minced beef, sausagemeat, half the onion, the egg, breadcrumbs, meat extract, herbs and seasoning for meatballs. Blend thoroughly and form into 16 balls.
2. Heat the lard in a pan and fry meatballs gently for 20 minutes, turning frequently. Drain on absorbent paper, then place in a serving dish and keep warm.
3. Meanwhile, heat butter in a pan and fry remaining onion and the celery for 5 minutes. Add tomatoes and simmer, uncovered, for 10 minutes, stirring occasionally.
4. Stir in tomato purée.
5. Blend cornflour and water and stir into sauce.
6. Bring to the boil, stirring.
7. Add half the soured cream and reheat, but do not boil.
8. Pour over meatballs and top with remaining soured cream.
9. Serve with hot buttered noodles.

VEAL ROLLS
Serves 4

4 veal fillets
2oz (50gm) soft white
breadcrumbs
1 tablespoon grated Parmesan
cheese
½ teaspoon Tabasco sauce
2 tablespoons chopped parsley
1 teaspoon salt
2 heaped teaspoons paprika
pepper
2 heaped teaspoons flour
1 tablespoon oil
1oz (25gm) butter
1 can (15oz or 387gm) tomato
juice

1. Put veal fillets between two
thicknesses of greaseproof paper
and beat out thinly.
2. Mix together the breadcrumbs,
cheese, Tabasco sauce, parsley
and salt and spread over the
fillets.
3. Roll up tightly and roll each
portion closely in foil or
greaseproof paper and secure.
Chill for about 1 hour.
4. Before cooking remove the
wrapping and, if necessary, tie
each roll with strong white
thread.
5. Mix the paprika pepper and
flour together and coat the rolls,
patting on gently.
6. Brown them lightly in hot oil
and butter in small flameproof
casserole.
7. Turn once, packing them as
closely as possible.
8. Add the tomato juice to cover
the rolls, cover casserole and
simmer until tender, about 30
minutes.
9. Blend rest of flour and paprika
pepper mixture with a little cold
water, pour some of the sauce
from the casserole into this and
blend smoothly.
10. Add to the casserole, boil for
3 minutes, stirring. Remove any
thread from rolls before serving.

ITALIAN PAPER-WRAPPED VEAL ESCALOPES
Serves 6

4oz (100gm) butter
6 thin slices roast ham, halved
2 tablespoons oil
6 veal escalopes about 4oz
(100gm) each
4oz (100gm) button mushrooms,
sliced
1oz (25gm) flour
¼ pint (125ml) beef stock
¼ pint (125ml) medium dry
white wine
1 small onion, chopped
2 teaspoons tomato purée
1 tablespoon chopped parsley
salt and freshly ground pepper

1. Preheat the oven to moderate
to moderately hot, 400 deg F or
gas 6 (200 deg C).
2. Thoroughly grease six pieces of
foil about 8 inches by 6 inches,
using half the butter, and place
a slice of ham in the centre of
each.
3. Heat the oil and remaining
butter and fry the escalopes for
2–3 minutes on each side.
4. Remove from the pan and set
aside. Add the mushrooms to the
pan and fry until browned.
5. Stir in the flour and cook for 1
minute.
6. Remove from the heat,
gradually add the stock, wine,
onion, tomato purée, parsley and
mushrooms and bring to the boil,
stirring continuously until
mixture thickens.
7. Season to taste and cool
slightly.
8. Spread a little of this sauce on
the ham, top with a veal escalope,
spread with the remaining sauce
and cover with a second slice of
ham.
9. Fold the foil or greaseproof
paper around the meat and press
the edges together to seal.
10. Place on a baking sheet and
bake for 15–20 minutes in the
centre of the oven.
11. It is the custom in Italy to
fold back the foil to serve these
escalopes.

VEAL ESCALOPES MARSALA
Serves 4

3½oz (87gm) butter
1lb (½ kilo) thin veal escalopes
flour to coat
salt and pepper
½ wine glass Marsala wine

1. Use a wide, deep frying pan.
Heat the butter until golden, then
place the veal slices, dusted with
flour, in the pan.
2. Cook on both sides over a high
heat.
3. Season with salt and pepper
and pour the Marsala wine over
the slices.
4. Cook for 1–2 minutes to allow
the flavour of the Marsala to
penetrate the meat.
5. Serve the escalopes in their
own sauce.

VEAL WITH TUNA FISH SAUCE
Serves 6

A popular Italian dish – *vitello tonnato*.

piece boned and rolled breast of veal (about 2½lb or 1¼ kilo)
10 anchovy fillets, cut in half
1 large carrot, peeled and cut in strips
8 gherkins
1 medium onion, peeled and sliced
2 sticks celery, chopped
thinly sliced rind of 1 lemon
5 tablespoons lemon juice
6 tablespoons dry white wine
3 tablespoons olive oil
½ pint (250ml) water
1 can (7oz or 175gm) tuna, drained
3 tablespoons veal stock
4 egg yolks
¾ pint (375ml) olive oil
salt
pickled onions, sliced, and capers to garnish

1. Using a sharp knife, make small cuts all over the meat and press in eight of the anchovy fillets.
2. Tie half the carrot strips and all the gherkins to the veal with thin string.
3. Place the veal in a saucepan and add the rest of the carrots, the onion, celery, lemon rind and 2 tablespoons juice, the wine, 3 tablespoons olive oil and water.
4. Simmer for 2 hours, or until tender. Take the veal out of the saucepan, discard the gherkins and carrots.
5. Place the veal in a bowl and strain the stock over it.
6. Set aside to cool. Discard the vegetables.
7. When cold, pour the stock into a saucepan and boil rapidly until reduced to about 3 tablespoons.
8. To make the sauce, pound the tuna and remaining anchovy fillets together to make a paste.
9. Stir in the reduced stock through fine sieve.
10. Place the egg yolks in a bowl and add the olive oil drop by drop, beating well to make a thick mayonnaise (or blend in a liquidizer).
11. Stir in the remaining lemon juice and tuna paste.
12. Cut the veal into thin slices and place on serving dish. Coat with some of the sauce and garnish with pickled onions and capers.
13. Serve cold, with the remaining sauce.

NORWEGIAN VEAL ROLLS
Serves 4

4 veal escalopes
4oz (100gm) butter, softened
2 level tablespoons chopped parsley
1 level teaspoon thyme
1 tablespoon lemon juice
2oz (50gm) butter
1½oz (37gm) flour
¾ pint (375ml) chicken stock
salt and pepper
¼ pint (125ml) single cream
parsley to garnish

1. Beat veal escalopes until they are thin.
2. Put softened butter into a basin. Add parsley, thyme and lemon juice and mix well together.
3. Spread a quarter of the mixture on each piece of veal.
4. Roll up and tie each with fine string.
5. Melt remaining butter in a large pan and brown the rolls on all sides.
6. Remove and keep warm.
7. Add flour to melted butter and cook for 1 minute.
8. Remove from heat and stir in the stock gradually.
9. Return to heat and bring to the boil, stirring. Season to taste.
10. Replace veal rolls and simmer gently, covered, for about 20 minutes.
11. When veal is cooked, remove from pan and place on serving dish.
12. Stir cream into sauce and heat through gently for 1–2 minutes, without boiling.
13. Pour over the veal rolls and garnish with parsley.

SWISS VEAL SLICES
Serves 4

4oz (100gm) spaghetti
4 veal fillets
juice of ½ lemon
1oz (25gm) flour, seasoned with salt and pepper
1 egg, beaten
2oz (50gm) cheese, grated
4oz (100gm) butter or margarine
grated cheese and parsley to garnish

1. Place the spaghetti in a saucepan of boiling, salted water and cook for 20–25 minutes.
2. Trim the veal and beat into thin slices.
3. Sprinkle with lemon juice and toss in the seasoned flour.
4. Mix the egg with the cheese and seasoning.
5. Place 1 dessertspoon of the cheese mixture on to one half of each veal slice and fold over. Secure with a wooden cocktail stick.
5. Melt 3oz (75gm) of the fat in a pan and fry the veal for 3–5 minutes on each side.
6. Drain the spaghetti and toss in the remaining butter. Place on a warm serving dish.
7. Remove the cocktail sticks and arrange the veal slices on the spaghetti.
8. Serve garnished with grated cheese and parsley.

WIENER SCHNITZEL
Serves 4

4 thin veal escalopes
½oz (12gm) flour, seasoned with
salt and pepper
1 egg, beaten
1 teaspoon oil
3oz (75gm) fine fresh
breadcrumbs
4oz (100gm) butter
2 tablespoons oil
4 lemon slices
4 gherkins
1 teaspoon capers
juice of 1 lemon
chopped parsley to garnish

1. Coat the escalopes with
seasoned flour, shake well, then
coat with the beaten egg mixed
with the oil, and the breadcrumbs.
2. Heat the butter in a large
frying pan and fry the escalopes
over a moderate heat for 5–10
minutes, turning once.
3. Drain and place on a large flat
dish and garnish each one with
lemon and gherkin slices and
capers.
4. Heat the lemon juice with the
butter remaining in the pan and
pour a little over each escalope.
5. Sprinkle with chopped parsley
and serve immediately.

DUTCH STUFFED VEAL
FILLETS
Serves 4

4oz (100gm) streaky bacon,
minced
2 tablespoons breadcrumbs
1 teaspoon chopped parsley
salt and pepper
nutmeg
1 egg, beaten
4 veal escalopes
1oz (25gm) butter
4 tablespoons stock

1. Mix bacon, breadcrumbs,
parsley and seasoning together
with the beaten egg.
2. Divide the mixture into four
and spread a little over each piece
of veal. Roll up and secure with
thin thread.
3. Heat the butter in a pan and
brown the rolls. Pour in the stock.
4. Cover and simmer for 30
minutes, or until tender.
5. Remove thread and serve.

CZECHOSLOVAKIAN STEW
WITH BREADCRUMB
DUMPLINGS
Serves 4

This recipe is equally delicious
made with chicken quarters. The
cooking time is then about 15
minutes longer.

8oz (200gm) carrots
4 sticks celery
1 tablespoon oil
1oz (25gm) butter
2 large onions, sliced, or 12
button onions
1¼lb (500gm) stewing veal
1oz (25gm) flour, seasoned with
salt and pepper
¾ pint (375ml) chicken stock
¼ teaspoon mace
1 tablespoon finely chopped
parsley
8oz (200gm) fresh white
breadcrumbs
4 tablespoons milk
2oz (50gm) butter or margarine
1 egg, beaten
½ teaspoon salt
pepper
finely grated rind and juice of
1 lemon

1. Preheat oven to moderate, 350
deg F or gas 4 (180 deg C).
2. Cut carrots and celery into
¼-inch slices.
3. Heat oil and 1oz (25gm) butter
in a large saucepan.
4. Add vegetables, cover and cook
gently, without browning, for
about 10 minutes.
5. Cut veal into ½-inch cubes, toss
in seasoned flour.
6. Add to vegetables and cook
until sealed, stirring frequently.
7. Add stock, mace and parsley
and bring to the boil.
8. Transfer to an ovenproof dish
and bake in the centre of the oven
for 45 minutes.
9. To make dumplings, soak
breadcrumbs in milk.
10. Soften butter then beat in
egg, soaked breadcrumbs, and salt
and pepper.
11. Shape into eight small balls.
12. Cook dumplings in boiling
salted water for 5 minutes. Drain
and add to stew about 10 minutes
before end of cooking time
together with the lemon rind and
juice.

ANDALUSIAN VEAL
Serves 4–6

This Spanish dish has a refreshing
orange flavour.

4 tablespoons oil
1 small onion, chopped
2lb (1 kilo) lean veal, cubed
1oz (25gm) flour
salt and black pepper
¾ pint (375ml) fresh orange
juice
3oz (75gm) raisins
3 tablespoons Angostura
bitters

1. Preheat oven to moderate to
moderately hot, 375 deg F or gas 5
(190 deg C).
2. Heat oil and gently fry onions
until opaque.
3. Dust veal with lightly seasoned
flour and add to onions.
4. Cook for several minutes until
outside of meat is sealed.
5. Add orange juice, raisins and
Angostura bitters; adjust
seasoning and cook in the centre
of the oven for 1 hour.

VEAL CACCIATORA
(Illustrated on page 36)
Serves 4–6

½oz (12gm) butter
1 medium onion, chopped
1 garlic clove, crushed
(optional)
1½lb (¾ kilo) lean pie veal, cut
in 1½-inch cubes
2 green peppers, blanched and
chopped
1 red pepper, blanched and
chopped
6 tomatoes, peeled and
quartered
salt and pepper
5oz (125gm) soured cream
2 tablespoons freshly chopped
parsley, and basil if available

1. Melt butter in pan and fry
onion gently for 3 minutes.
2. Add garlic if liked.
3. Add veal and fry gently for a
further 3 minutes.
4. Stir in peppers and tomatoes
and bring gently to boil, stirring
continuously.
5. Season, cover and simmer
gently for 1½ hours, until veal is
cooked.
6. Before serving, stir in soured
cream and herbs and reheat
without boiling.
6. Serve with plain boiled rice.

OSSO BUCO
Serves 4–6

A traditional Italian dish.

3–4lb (1½–2 kilo) shin of veal
flour
6 tablespoons olive oil
1 medium onion, thinly sliced
1 medium carrot, grated
1 stick celery, chopped
8 tomatoes, skinned and
chopped
1 level tablespoon tomato
purée
¼ pint (125ml) white wine
¼ pint (125ml) chicken or beef
stock
salt and pepper
dash of Tabasco sauce
finely grated rind of 1 lemon
finely chopped parsley
1 garlic clove, chopped

1. Ask the butcher to saw the veal
shin into 3-inch pieces. Coat in
flour.
2. Heat oil in large pan, add veal
pieces, a few at a time, and fry
until well browned.
3. Remove veal and add onion,
carrot and celery to oil remaining
in pan and fry slowly until soft
but not brown.
5. Stir in tomatoes, purée, wine,
stock, salt and pepper and
Tabasco sauce. Bring to the boil.
6. Replace veal, lower heat and
cover pan. Simmer gently until
tender about 1½–2 hours.
7. Turn on to a warm dish and
sprinkle with lemon rind, parsley
and garlic mixed well together.

DUTCH VEAL WITH CREAM SAUCE
Serves 4

4 veal escalopes
salt and pepper
2oz (50gm) butter
4 thin slices Gouda cheese
4 bacon rashers
¼ pint (125ml) double cream
1 tablespoon tomato purée
½ teaspoon sugar

1. Preheat oven to moderate to
moderately hot, 400 deg F or gas 6
(200 deg C).
2. Beat the veal thinly and season
with salt and pepper.
3. Fry in butter on both sides for
about 7 minutes altogether.
4. Remove from pan and drain on
absorbent paper.
5. On each escalope place a slice
of Gouda cheese and top with a
bacon rasher.
6. Place in an ovenproof dish and
cook in the centre of the oven for
15 minutes.
7. Blend the cream with the
tomato purée and sugar, pour
around the veal and cook for a
further 5 minutes.

CHOPKEBAB
Serves 4–6

Kebabs in the Bulgarian style.

2lb (1 kilo) lean lamb or veal
1 can (10oz or 250gm) tomato
juice
1½lb (¾ kilo) marrow
salt
paprika pepper
6oz (150gm) butter
dill
rosemary

1. Remove any bones from the
meat and cut into cubes.
2. Sprinkle with salt and soak for
30 minutes in the tomato juice.
3. Thread pieces of marrow and
lamb on to skewers.
4. Sprinkle with salt and paprika
pepper. Fry in half the butter for
about 5 minutes.
5. Remove from pan, dip in the
tomato juice again, and then fry
until well browned in the
remaining butter.
6. Sprinkle with finely chopped
dill and rosemary.

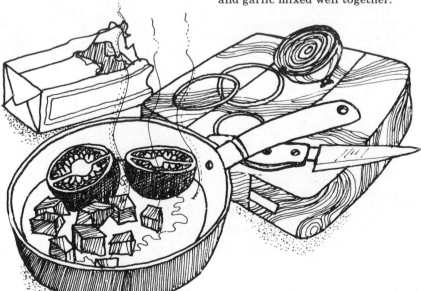

MOUSSAKA
Serves 4

A well-known dish from Greece.

1lb ($\frac{1}{2}$ kilo) aubergines, thinly
sliced
oil for frying
2 large onions, thinly sliced
1 garlic clove, crushed
1lb ($\frac{1}{2}$ kilo) minced lamb
1 can (15oz or 375gm) tomatoes
2 tablespoons tomato purée
dash of Tabasco sauce
salt and pepper
2 eggs
1 carton (5oz or 125gm) single
cream
2oz (50gm) Cheddar cheese,
grated
1oz (25gm) Parmesan cheese,
grated

1. Preheat oven to moderate, 350
deg F or gas 4 (180 deg C).
2. Fry the aubergines in oil for
3–4 minutes; remove and drain
well.
3. Fry the onions and garlic in 1
tablespoon of oil until pale golden
brown.
4. Add the lamb and cook for
about 10 minutes, stirring
occasionally.
5. Add the tomatoes, tomato
purée and Tabasco sauce and mix
well.
6. Bring to the boil and simmer
for 20–25 minutes. Season with
salt and pepper.
7. Arrange alternate layers of
aubergines and lamb mixture in a
large soufflé dish or shallow
casserole.
8. Bake in the centre of the oven
for 35–40 minutes.
9. Meanwhile, beat the eggs and
cream together and stir in the
cheeses. Pour on to the moussaka
and return to the oven for 15–20
minutes until well risen and
golden brown.

NEAPOLITAN LAMB CHOPS
(Illustrated on page 36)
Serves 4

4 best end neck of lamb chops
3 tablespoons chutney
1 tablespoon clear honey
$\frac{1}{2}$ teaspoon mixed herbs
1 tablespoon made mustard
1 beef stock cube
salt and pepper

1. Place the chops in a frying pan.
2. Mix together the chutney,
honey, herbs, mustard and the
crumbled stock cube. Season, and
spoon half this mixture over the
chops.
3. Fry the chops in their own fat
for 15 minutes.
4. Turn chops over and spread
them with the remaining mixture,
cooking for a further 15 minutes.

CRUSTY ROAST LAMB
Serves 4

1 small leg of lamb (2$\frac{1}{2}$–3lb or
1$\frac{1}{4}$–1$\frac{1}{2}$ kilo)
1 garlic clove
2oz (50gm) soft white
breadcrumbs
3 tablespoons chopped parsley
1 level teaspoon mixed herbs
1oz (25gm) butter
2 teaspoons English mustard
lemon juice

1. Preheat oven to moderate to
moderately hot, 375 deg F or gas 5
(190 deg C) – see stage 6.
2. Trim the joint, removing as
much fat as possible from the top.
3. Cut the garlic into small
slivers. Make several small, deep
incisions all over the lamb and
insert a sliver of garlic into each.
4. Place the breadcrumbs, parsley
and mixed herbs in a bowl.
5. Melt the butter in a small pan,
stir in the mustard and pour on to
the breadcrumbs etc. Mix together
and spread all over the top and
sides of the joint, pressing well
down with your hands.
6. Sprinkle liberally with lemon
juice and leave for 2 hours, in a
cool place, before cooking.
7. Roast in the centre of the oven
for 1$\frac{1}{2}$ hours.

SHISH KEBAB
Serves 4–5

Kebabs are said to be Turkish in
origin, created by Ottoman
soldiers and cooked over their
camp fires. Now they are served
in many Eastern European
countries.

4 tomatoes
4 tablespoons olive oil
1 large onion, peeled and
grated
2 bayleaves
2 level teaspoons dried
marjoram or oregano
1 level teaspoon salt
freshly milled pepper
2lb (1 kilo) lamb fillet, cut into
1-inch pieces
1 large onion
2 green peppers

1. Quarter the tomatoes and
scoop out the pulp.
2. Place the pulp in a sieve and
press to extract the juice.
3. Mix the juice with the oil,
grated onion, bayleaves,
marjoram or oregano, salt and
pepper. Marinate the lamb in this
mixture for at least 3 hours.
4. Thread pieces of meat, onion
and green pepper alternately on
to skewers and cook under a hot
grill for 7–8 minutes, turning
frequently.
5. Baste with the remaining
marinade while cooking. Serve
hot with cucumber salad (see page
32) and rice.

KEBABS WITH CRUSADERS' SAUCE
Serves 4

A special recipe from the Cyprus Hilton.

4 tablespoons olive oil
1¼ teaspoons Tabasco sauce
salt
1lb (½ kilo) lamb fillet or rump steak, cut in 1-inch cubes
8 button mushrooms
½oz (12gm) butter
1 medium onion, chopped
1 garlic clove, finely chopped
1 small red pepper, chopped
1oz (25gm) gherkins, chopped
2 level teaspoons flour
¼ pint (125ml) beef stock
2 tablespoons brandy
2 tablespoons double cream

1. Mix together olive oil, 1 teaspoon Tabasco sauce and the salt. Pour over the steak and leave to marinate for about 2 hours.
2. Arrange steak and mushrooms on four kebab skewers, brush well with remaining marinade and grill for 10–15 minutes.
3. Meanwhile prepare sauce, melt butter and fry onion, garlic and red pepper until tender but not brown.
4. Add gherkins and flour. Mix well.
5. Remove from heat and gradually stir in stock.
6. Return to heat, bring to the boil, stirring and cook for 1 minute.
7. Add remaining Tabasco sauce. Stir in brandy and cream.
8. Heat through but do not boil. Serve sauce with kebabs.

SWEDISH HASH
Serves 4

12oz (300gm) cooked pork or beef
2 large potatoes, partly cooked
1oz (25gm) butter
1 tablespoon oil
1 large onion, chopped
salt and freshly ground pepper
4 eggs
butter for frying

1. Dice the meat and potatoes.
2. Heat the butter with half the oil and fry the onion until soft.
3. Remove from the pan and put aside.
4. Add the remaining oil to the pan and fry the meat and potatoes until lightly browned.
5. Add the fried onion, and salt and pepper to taste.
6. Transfer to a heated serving dish and top with an egg fried in butter for each person. (Hash is always served with pickled beetroots in Sweden.)

PORK A LA FLAMANDE
Serves 6

piece pork shoulder (about 2lb or 1 kilo)
1 garlic clove, slivered
salt and pepper
2 medium onions, quartered
¼ pint (125ml) apple juice or beer
6 potatoes, peeled and cubed
6 carrots, peeled and sliced
1 turnip, peeled and cubed

1. Make several slits in meat and insert slivers of garlic.
2. Brown meat on all sides in its own fat.
3. Sprinkle with salt and pepper, add onions and liquid.
4. Cover and cook slowly until almost tender, about 1½ hours, adding more liquid if needed.
5. Add vegetables, cover and cook until meat and vegatables are tender, about 30 minutes.
6. If liked, thicken liquid with 1 tablespoon flour blended with a little liquid.

PORK CARBONNADE
Serves 4–6

1oz (25gm) lard
2 leeks, chopped
1 garlic clove, crushed
1¼lb (500gm) shoulder pork, in 1-inch squares
2oz (50gm) flour
seasoning
½ pint (250ml) brown ale
bouquet garni
Tabasco sauce
grated rind of 1 lemon
3oz (75gm) small mushrooms

1. Melt lard in a flameproof casserole, and fry leeks and garlic for a few minutes.
2. Toss pork in seasoned flour, add to leeks and fry for 5 minutes.
3. Add ale, bouquet garni, Tabasco sauce, lemon rind and mushrooms.
4. Bring to the boil, cover and simmer for 1¼ hours.

BAECKAOFFA
Serves 4–6

8oz (200gm) pork shoulder
8oz (200gm) lamb leg or shoulder
1lb (½ kilo) lean chuck steak
½ pint (250ml) Sylvaner wine
pinch of thyme
salt and pepper
1 small bayleaf
1 tablespoon chopped parsley
1oz (25gm) butter
4 large onions, sliced
4 large potatoes, sliced

1. Cut meats into 2-inch pieces and place in a large bowl.
2. Pour over the wine and seasonings and leave to marinate overnight.
3. Preheat oven to moderate, 350 deg F or gas 4 (180 deg C).
4. Grease a large casserole with the butter and then make a layer of onions and potatoes on the bottom, then layer the combined meats. Repeat until casserole is full.
5. Pour over marinade. Cover and place in the oven for 1½ hours.

NASI GORENG
Serves 4–6

An Indonesian dish brought to Holland by Dutch colonists from the East and now one of Holland's national dishes.

8oz (200gm) long-grain rice
8oz (200gm) onions
4oz (100gm) butter
12oz (300gm) pork shoulder
12oz (300gm) mixed cooked vegetables
salt and pepper
1 level teaspoon curry powder
2 tablespoons soy sauce
1 egg (see method) and tomato wedges to garnish

1. Cook rice in boiling salted water for approximately 12 minutes.
2. Turn into a sieve and separate the grains by refreshing with cold running water, until surplus starch is removed. Allow to drain.
3. Cut onions into rings and fry in half the butter with cubed pork.
4. Cook for about 20 minutes on medium heat, browning slowly.
5. Add remaining butter, rice, mixed vegetables, salt, pepper, curry powder and soy sauce.
6. Blend well over the heat until very hot. Beat the egg for the garnish and cook it, like a pancake, in a little oil. Cut into thin strips.
7. Turn pork mixture into an ovenproof dish and garnish with omelette strips and tomato wedges.
8. Place under a hot grill for a few minutes and then serve with peanuts, shrimp crisps and a green salad.

PORK LOIN WITH APRICOT STUFFING
Serves 6–8

1 boned pork loin (about 5lb or 2½ kilo)
6oz (150gm) dried apricots
½oz (12gm) butter
2 medium onions, finely chopped
3oz (75gm) breadcrumbs
1 lemon
1 teaspoon dried rosemary
3 teaspoons dry mustard
salt and black pepper

1. Preheat oven to moderate to moderately hot, 400 deg F or gas 6 (200 deg C).
2. Just cover the apricots with cold water, bring to the boil and simmer for 5 minutes.
3. Drain the apricots and cut into strips.
4. Melt butter in a pan and fry the onions until soft.
5. Mix the onion, apricot strips and the breadcrumbs together.
6. Add the grated lemon rind and the juice, the rosemary and 1 teaspoon mustard.
7. Season well with salt and black pepper.
8. Spread the joint with the stuffing, roll up and secure firmly with string or skewers.
9. Rub the loin all over with remaining mustard – this ensures a crisp, well-flavoured crackling.
9. Roast for 2 hours basting occasionally with the pan juices.

DUTCH PORK CHOPS WITH CHEESE SAUCE
Serves 4

4 pork chops, trimmed
1½oz (37gm) butter
½oz (12gm) flour
½ pint (250ml) milk
4oz (100gm) Gouda cheese, grated
4oz (100gm) button mushrooms

1. Preheat oven to hot, 425 deg F or gas 7 (220 deg C).
2. Fry the pork chops in 1oz (25gm) butter for 5–10 minutes.
3. Meanwhile make a cheese sauce with the remaining butter, the flour, milk and 3oz (75gm) cheese (see Basic recipes, page 100).
4. Remove the pork chops from the pan and place in a casserole. Fry the mushrooms.
5. Place a few mushrooms on each pork chop, pour over the cheese sauce and sprinkle with the rest of the cheese.
6. Cook in the centre of the oven for 30 minutes.

TIPSY PORK
Serves 6

A recipe from Tuscany using Chianti wine.

6 pork chops
salt and pepper
2oz (50gm) butter
1 garlic clove
sprigs of parsley
pinch of fennel seed
¼ bottle Chianti Classico

1. Sprinkle the pork chops with salt and pepper and fry them, in butter, over a moderate heat with the chopped garlic, parsley and fennel seed.
2. When the chops are golden brown pour off excess fat; pour the wine over and continue cooking over a low heat until the wine has almost evaporated.

DANISH CHRISTMAS HAM
Serves 4–5

1 can (1lb or ½ kilo) ham
1 tablespoon made mustard
3 tablespoons demerara sugar
2oz (50gm) butter

1. Preheat oven to hot, 425 deg F or gas 7 (220 deg C).
2. Remove any jelly from the ham. Spread mustard evenly over the top and sides.
3. Place ham in baking tin, press sugar on top and sides and put knobs of butter on top.
4. Place the ham on the middle shelf of the oven and cook for 20 minutes – until sugar and butter mixture is crisp.
5. This is served in Denmark hot or cold with golden potatoes and Danish sweet sour red cabbage (see pages 67 and 70).

POLISH STYLE GAMMON AND APPLE
Serves 4–6

2 thick gammon rashers (each about 8oz or 200gm)
cloves
2 tablespoons brown sugar
½ pint (250ml) sweet cider, or cooking sherry and water
6 small cooking apples

1. Preheat oven to hot, 425 deg F of gas 7 (220 deg C).
2. Snip the rind of the rashers all round, to prevent curling of the gammon during cooking.
3. Put in an ovenproof dish, inserting a few cloves in the slits in the rind, sprinkle with the brown sugar and pour over the cider or sherry and water.
4. Cook in the oven for 10 minutes.
5. Peel core and slice the apples.
6. Take rashers from oven, arrange the apples on the top, replace and cook for a further 35 minutes until apples are soft. Serve rashers with hot vegetables.

STUFFED GAMMON RASHERS
Serves 6

1 small packet frozen spinach
½ onion, chopped
4oz (100gm) sausagemeat
3 tablespoons fresh breacrumbs
2 tablespoons lemon juice
salt and pepper
6 unsmoked gammon rashers
oil or fat for cooking
stock

1. Preheat oven to moderate to moderately hot, 375 deg F or gas 5 (190 deg C).
2. Cook and drain spinach and mix with onion, sausagemeat, breadcrumbs, lemon juice and seasoning.
3. Spread a little of the mixture on each rasher, roll up lengthways and secure with thread.
4. Brown in hot oil.
5. Transfer to casserole dish, pour in a little stock and cook, covered, for 45 minutes.

LIVER TYROLEAN STYLE
Serves 4–6

An Austrian substantial snack dish.

8oz (200gm) calf's liver
3oz (75gm) butter
4oz (100gm) button mushrooms, sliced
4 tablespoons dry white wine
2 level teaspoons cornflour
4 level tablespoons soured cream
salt and pepper
4–6 slices buttered toast
chopped parsley to garnish

1. Cut liver into thin strips, about 2 inches long.
2. Melt butter in a small pan, add liver and cook gently for about 2 minutes.
3. Add mushrooms and 3 tablespoons of the wine.
4. Continue cooking gently for about 10 minutes.
5. Blend cornflour with remaining wine and stir into the liver and mushrooms.
6. Cook for 1 minute, stirring. Remove from heat, add soured cream and seasoning.
7. Serve on buttered toast; garnish with parsley.

STUFFED CALF'S LIVER A TRANSMONTANA
(Illustrated on page 36)
Serves 4

A traditional Portuguese way of serving liver.

1lb (½ kilo) calf's liver, sliced
3 hard-boiled eggs, sliced
5oz (125gm) lean smoked ham
1 garlic clove, crushed
1 sprig parsley
1 teaspoon salt and freshly ground pepper
2oz (50gm) butter
1 medium onion, chopped
3 egg yolks
juice of half a lemon

1. Preheat oven to moderate to moderately hot, 375 deg F or gas 5 (190 deg C).
2. Place on each slice of liver, equal portions of egg, chopped ham, a little garlic, chopped parsley, salt and pepper.
3. Roll up the liver round its filling and skewer or tie with string.
4. Heat the butter in a frying pan and fry the onion until tender. Add 3 tablespoons water.
5. Place the liver in a baking tin or dish and pour over the onion mixture and cook in the centre of the oven for 15–20 minutes.
7. Remove from the oven, cover with scrambled eggs, made with the egg yolks and the lemon juice.

TRIPE A LA MODE DE CAEN
Serves 6–8

**2lb (1 kilo) tripe, in 1-inch
squares
1 cow heel or 2 calf's feet, cut
in 1-inch pieces
4 leeks, chopped
2 large onions, chopped
bouquet garni of 2 bayleaves,
3 cloves, 2 sprigs of thyme
1 pint (approximately ½ litre)
cider or dry white wine
2 tablespoons brandy
salt and pepper
2 teaspoons chopped parsley**

1. Preheat oven to cool, 300 deg F
or gas 2 (150 deg C).
2. Put all the ingredients, except
the parsley, with water to cover,
in a large casserole and cover
tightly.
3. Cook in the centre of the oven
for 4 hours.
4. Remove the bouquet garni and
sprinkle with chopped parsley
before serving.

KIDNEYS IN WINE AND MUSTARD SAUCE
Serves 4

**12 lambs' kidneys
3oz (75gm) butter
1 tablespoon finely chopped
onion
¼ pint (125ml) dry white wine
1 tablespoon lemon juice
1½ tablespoons French mustard
chopped parsley to garnish**

1. Skin the kidneys, remove any
fat but leave whole.
2. Heat 2oz (50gm) butter in a
frying pan.
3. Fry the kidneys in the hot
butter for 5 minutes, turning
frequently. Do not overcook. The
kidneys should stiffen and brown
slightly without becoming hard
and dry. Remove and keep warm.
4. Add the onion to the frying
pan and cook for 1–2 minutes
until soft and transparent.
5. Add the wine and lemon juice,
raise heat and boil until the
liquid has reduced by half.
6. Mix the mustard and
remaining butter and swirl this
into the sauce, in spoonfuls, off
the heat.
7. Slice the kidneys and replace
in pan together with any of their
juices.
8. Toss over low heat for 1–2
minutes, but do not reboil.
9. Garnish with chopped parsley.

ARAGON CHICKEN
Serves 4

**1 large onion, peeled and
chopped
2 garlic cloves, chopped
4 tablespoons oil
1lb (½ kilo) tomatoes, peeled
salt and pepper
2 oven-ready chickens (each
about 2lb or 1 kilo), halved
8oz (200gm) ham, cut in small
strips
3 red peppers, chopped
1 teaspoon chopped parsley**

1. Fry the onion and 1 garlic
clove in half the oil until soft.
2. Add the tomatoes, salt and
pepper and simmer gently for
20–25 minutes, or until the
tomatoes have become pulpy.
3. Meanwhile, heat the remaining
oil and garlic and brown the
chicken halves on both sides.
4. Add the ham and cook until
browned.
5. Add the tomato sauce, red
peppers and parsley.
6. Cover and simmer gently for
about 40 minutes, or until the
chicken is cooked.

CHICKEN TETRAZZINI
Serves 4

**6oz (150gm) spaghetti
1½ pints (approximately ¾ litre)
chicken stock
4 tablespoons oil
1 green pepper, finely chopped
8oz (200gm) onions, finely
chopped
8oz (200gm) mushrooms, finely
chopped
1 chicken, cooked and cubed
1 tablespoon chopped pimentos
salt and freshly ground pepper
2oz (50gm) butter
1oz (25gm) flour
½ pint (250ml) milk
4 tablespoons sherry
1½oz (37gm) Parmesan cheese,
grated**

1. Cook spaghetti in boiling
chicken stock until tender,
approximately 25 minutes. Drain.
2. Heat the oil and fry the green
pepper, onions and mushrooms
for 3 minutes, add the chicken,
pimentos, salt and pepper; keep
on a low heat.
3. To make the sauce, heat the
butter in a saucepan and add the
flour, stirring well. Cook for
1 minute without browning.
4. Gradually add the milk,
constantly stirring and cook for
1 minute.
5. Add the salt, pepper, sherry
and spaghetti to the chicken
mixture, together with the sauce.
Stir well.
6. Sprinkle with Parmesan
cheese, cover and simmer for 15
minutes.

BELGIAN BRAISED CHICORY CASSEROLE WITH CHICKEN
Serves 4

2oz (50gm) butter
1 teaspoon salt and pepper
4 heads chicory
4 tablespoons water
4 large slices roast chicken
4 tablespoons white Bordeaux wine

1. Preheat oven to moderate, 350 deg F or gas 4 (180 deg C).
2. Place butter in heavy pan or casserole and melt over medium heat. Add seasoning.
3. Place each washed and dried chicory head in pan.
4. Brown chicory lightly for 2 minutes each side.
5. Add the water and allow chicory to simmer, uncovered for 15 minutes.
6. Remove from heat. Place chicken slices over chicory; pour wine over the chicken.
7. Cover casserole and place in oven for 10 minutes, or until chicken is heated through.
8. If liked, this can be served on buttered toast.

QUICK COQ AU VIN
Serves 4

A quick way of making this traditional French casserole.

4 frozen chicken portions
2oz (50gm) dripping
4oz (100gm) mushrooms, sliced
2 small onions, chopped
1 large can tomato soup
½ pint (250ml) water or chicken stock
fried bread triangles and chopped parsley to garnish

1. Trim and wipe the chicken and fry gently in the dripping for 3–5 minutes.
2. Add the mushrooms and onions to the pan and continue frying for 2–3 minutes.
3. Remove chicken from pan and stir in the soup.
4. Pour the stock and wine into the pan and replace chicken in sauce.
5. Cover the pan and simmer for 25–30 minutes, stirring occasionally.
6. Serve garnished with triangles of fried bread and parsley.

RUMANIAN CHICKEN VINAIGRETTE
Serves 4

1 chicken, quartered, or 4 frozen chicken quarters
2 tablespoons olive oil
2–3 medium onions
½oz (12gm) flour
about ¼ pint (125ml) stock or water
2 tablespoons tomato purée
2 garlic cloves
1 bayleaf
6–8 peppercorns
salt
4 tablespoons wine or vinegar

1. Brown the chicken quarters in hot oil. Remove.
2. Slice onions thinly and fry until golden brown, add the flour and mix well.
3. Add the water or stock, tomato purée, crushed garlic, bayleaf, peppercorns and salt to taste.
4. Stir well and add the chicken joints; cook slowly with the lid on saucepan until chicken is tender.
5. Stir frequently and add more hot water or stock if necessary.
6. When nearly cooked add the wine or vinegar and simmer for a further 10–15 minutes.

POULET PAPRIKA
Serves 4–5

1 roasting chicken (about 3lb or 1½ kilo)
flour, seasoned with salt and pepper
1oz (25gm) butter
1 tablespoon oil
1 medium onion, chopped
1 garlic clove, crushed
1 large green pepper, thinly sliced
1 large red pepper, thinly sliced
4 tomatoes, de-seeded and chopped
1 level tablespoon paprika pepper
salt and pepper
¼ pint (125ml) chicken stock

1. Preheat oven to very moderate, 325 deg F or gas 3 (170 deg C).
2. Cut chicken into eight serving pieces; coat in seasoned flour and fry in the butter and oil until lightly browned.
3. Place joints in a casserole

4. Fry onion until soft, add remaining ingredients and bring to the boil.
5. Pour over chicken, cook in the centre of the oven for 1½ hours.

CHICKEN CHASSEUR MARENGO
(Illustrated on page 36)
Serves 4

4 chicken breasts
1oz (25gm) butter
1 tablespoon oil
2 shallots or small onions, finely chopped
½oz (12gm) flour
2 tablespoons dry sherry
½ pint (250ml) chicken stock
2 level tablespoons tomato purée
4oz (100gm) button mushrooms, sliced
2 teaspoons lemon juice
seasoning
croûtons to garnish

1. Fry chicken breasts in the butter and oil for 15 minutes, or until cooked through.
2. Drain and keep warm on a serving dish.
3. Fry the shallots or onions in the pan, stir in the flour and blend in the remaining ingredients.
4. Bring to the boil, stirring, and simmer for 10 minutes.
5. Adjust seasoning and pour sauce over chicken.
6. Garnish with croûtons and serve with boiled rice.

Valencia paella (see page 62)   Cod Palermo (see page 58)

Lasagne with yogurt topping (see page 65)   Italian ham and pasta shells (see page 65)

Algarve beans (see page 67) Danish sweet sour red cabbage (see page 70)
Melon Copenhagen (see page 79) Italian stuffed baked oranges (see page 81)

DUCKLING WITH CHERRY SAUCE
Serves 3–4

1 duckling (about 4–5lb or 2–2½ kilo)
½ lemon
sprig of thyme
salt and pepper
1 can (1lb or ½ kilo) stoned black cherries
1 level tablespoon cornflour
salt and pepper
1 miniature bottle Cherry Heering
lemon slices and watercress sprigs to garnish

1. Preheat oven to moderate, 350 deg F or gas 4 (180 deg C).
2. Remove giblets from duckling. Place the half lemon and thyme inside the body of bird. Season with salt and pepper.
2. Prick the skin all over, taking care not to pierce the flesh.
4. Weigh and roast allowing 25 minutes per lb (½ kilo).
5. Prick once during cooking.
6. Place giblets in small pan, cover with water and cook gently for 20 minutes.
7. Drain the cherries, make the juice up to ½ pint (250ml) with the giblet stock.
8. Remove duck on to serving dish and keep hot. Reserve the lemon. Strain fat off into bowl.
9. Blend a little of the juice and stock with the cornflour. Add this to the pan and bring to the boil, stirring.
10. Cook until sauce clears.
11. Add Cherry Heering and half the cherries.
12. Squeeze in lemon juice.
13. Garnish duck with lemon slices, watercress sprigs and remaining cherries. Serve the sauce separately.

PARTRIDGES COOKED IN THE SPANISH STYLE
Serves 4

oil for frying
4 partridges
3 onions, chopped
3 garlic cloves
cloves
peppercorns
bayleaf
thyme
salt
¾ pint (375ml) white wine
about 4 tablespoons vinegar

1. Heat the oil in a frying pan and brown the cleaned partidges quickly over a high heat.
2. When golden, remove to a casserole.
3. Brown the chopped onions in the same oil, then add them with the oil to the partridges.
4. Add the finely chopped garlic, cloves, peppercorns, bayleaf, thyme and salt.
5. Add the white wine and vinegar. (The liquid should almost cover the birds.)
6. Cover tightly and simmer until tender.
7. Arrange partridges on a heated serving dish and keep warm. Reduce the cooking liquid by rapid boiling, then spoon over the partridges.

MILD MUSTARD SAUCE

A favourite German sauce.

2oz (50gm) butter
2oz (50gm) flour
1 pint (approximately ½ litre) milk
1½ level tablespoons German mustard
pinch of nutmeg
salt and pepper

1. Melt butter in a saucepan, add flour and cook for a minute.
2. Remove from heat, and stir in milk gradually.
3. Return to heat and bring to the boil, stirring.
4. Cook for 1 minute and stir in the mustard, nutmeg and seasonings.
5. Serve hot with gammon or ham.

PIRI-PIRI SAUCE

A typical Portuguese piquant sauce, excellent with chicken, pork or shellfish – brush it over the food before grilling.

4–6 small chillies
½ pint (250ml) olive oil
1 bayleaf
small piece lemon peel

1. Preheat oven to very cool, 225 deg F or gas ¼ (110 deg C).
2. Take the top off each chilli with a sharp knife then put them in the olive oil in an ovenproof dish.
2. Add bayleaf and lemon rind and set the mixture to infuse for several hours at the bottom of the oven.
3. Cool, seal and store for at least 24 hours before using.

TOMATO SAUCE

1 onion, finely chopped
½ garlic clove
2 tablespoons olive oil
1 can tomatoes
salt and pepper
1 bayleaf

1. Fry onion and garlic in olive oil in a thick-bottomed saucepan (do not allow to brown).
2. Add the tomatoes, salt, pepper and bayleaf.
3. Simmer, uncovered for about 30 minutes.
4. Blend in a liquidizer or press through a sieve.
5. Serve with chicken, beef or pasta.

Fish, pasta and vegetables

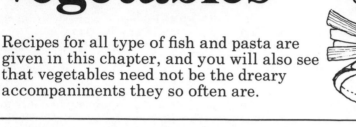

Recipes for all type of fish and pasta are given in this chapter, and you will also see that vegetables need not be the dreary accompaniments they so often are.

Fresh fish is one of the joys of eating in Mediterranean countries; sardines grilled on the beach in Portugal; red mullet in Spain; fish kebabs in Eastern Mediterranean countries. Seafood too: lobsters, shrimps and scampi often served with rice as in paella, Spain's most renowned dish. But all around western Europe, the king fish is cod, particularly beloved in Norway and Sweden where recipes can be rich and elaborate. The Bergen housewife buys her cod live and rushes home to cook it at its freshest. It is often served plain with melted butter and boiled potatoes. In Spain and Portugal, cod is cooked with tomatoes, oil and garlic. But in Norway and further south in Portugal, Spain and Italy dried cod is used as a basis for dishes; this stems from the days when it was the only way of preserving fish.

Pasta and rice are part of the staple diet of Italians with many more variations on the theme than just the well-known spaghetti bolognaise.

The Continental housewife has marvellous ideas for preparing vegetables, other than boiling them. I have given some of these ways in this chapter to add variety of taste and choice of vegetables to meat or fish courses, or even to serve on their own between courses.

PRINCE'S FISH
Serves 4

A dish served, according to Norwegian legend, to a prince who arrived in a town where all the chef had was cod. Hence the name *prinsfisk*.

2½oz (62gm) butter
salt and pepper
4 cod cutlets
4oz (100gm) shrimps or prawns
1 small can asparagus tips, drained
1oz (25gm) flour
½ pint (250ml) milk
2 tablespoons sherry
small cooked pastry shapes or potato crisps and lemon slices to garnish

1. Heat 1½oz (37gm) of the butter in a frying pan and fry the seasoned fish on both sides.
2. Top the fish with half the prawns and the asparagus tips and cook through. Arrange on a serving dish and keep warm.
3. Meanwhile, make the sauce with the remaining butter, the flour and milk. Add the rest of the prawns, sherry and seasoning.
4. Pour the sauce between the cutlets of fish. Garnish with the pastry shapes or crisps and lemon slices.

COD PORTUGUESE
Serves 6

2oz (50gm) butter
1 onion, finely chopped
6 cod steaks or cutlets
½ pint (250ml) white wine
juice of half a lemon
seasoning
2 tablespoons tomato purée
1 large can tomatoes
1 green pepper, blanched and chopped
1 tablespoon chopped chervil or parsley
8 stuffed olives, sliced
2 pears, peeled, cored and thickly sliced

1. Butter a large shallow cooking pan. Scatter in the chopped onion and place cod steaks in pan.
2. Pour over the white wine and lemon juice, and season to taste.
3. Cover with a piece of buttered greaseproof paper and poach for 10–15 minutes.
4. Remove fish steaks from pan and rapidly reduce the cooking liquor.
5. Add the tomato purée, tomatoes, green pepper, chopped chervil and olives. Simmer for 5 minutes.
6. Add sliced pears and simmer a further 5 minutes. Add fish steaks to sauce and heat through gently. Serve at once.

ITALIAN FISH SAVOURY
Serves 4

1 onion, chopped
1 garlic clove, crushed
4oz (100gm) mushrooms, sliced
1oz (25gm) butter
1 can (15oz or 375gm)
mushroom soup
6oz (150gm) cooked pasta shells
(raw weight)
1 large packet cod steaks,
cooked and flaked
3 tomatoes, chopped
½ medium can pineapple pieces,
drained
2 tablespoons peanuts
salt and pepper
parsley and croûtons to
garnish

1. Fry the onion, garlic and
mushrooms in butter for 5
minutes.
2. Add the soup, heat through
then stir in the other ingredients,
except the garnish.
3. Cook gently for a few minutes
then pile into a dish and garnish
with parsley and croûtons.

DUTCH COD STEAKS WITH SPINACH
Serves 4

1 large packet frozen cod
fillets, thawed and skinned
2–3 bread slices, crusts
removed and soaked in milk
1 small onion, chopped and
lightly fried
salt and pepper
nutmeg
flour
1 egg yolk
breadcrumbs
butter and oil for frying
1 packet (11oz or 275gm) frozen
chopped spinach, cooked
3–4 anchovy fillets, chopped

1. Chop the fish finely and mix
with the soaked bread, onion,
salt, pepper and nutmeg.
2. Shape the mixture into rissoles,
dip in flour, egg yolk and
breadcrumbs.
3. Fry gently in butter and oil for
10–15 minutes, until golden
brown. Drain on absorbent
paper.
4. Serve on a bed of chopped
spinach mixed with the anchovies.

SWEET FISH FROM ITALY
Serves 6

This recipe is supposed to have
been inspired by Catherine de
Medici who loved fish so much
she had it brought to France
from Italy, poached in kegs of
honey.

1½lb (¾ kilo) cod fillet or 6 cod
steaks
salt and pepper
flour
oil for frying
1 teaspoon rosemary
2 tablespoons honey
juice of 2 lemons
2 tablespoons pine nuts
(optional)
1 garlic clove, crushed
¼ pint (125ml) water
2 tablespoons raisins

1. If using cod fillet, cut the fish
into large pieces. (Leave cod
steaks whole).
2. Season the fish with salt and
pepper and roll lightly in flour.
3. Fry in a little hot oil to which
the rosemary has been added.
4. Place the fish in a fireproof
dish.
5. Place all the other ingredients
in a small pan, bring to the boil,
pour over the fish and simmer
gently for 5 minutes.

NORWEGIAN COD
Serves 4

½oz (12gm) margarine
2 tablespoons milk
1 tablespoon lemon juice
1 packet (14oz or 350gm)
frozen cod steaks, thawed
finely grated rind of 1 small
lemon
salt and pepper
3 tomatoes, skinned and
quartered

1. Melt the margarine in a pan,
add the milk and lemon juice and
place the cod steaks in the
liquid.
2. Sprinkle over grated lemon
rind, and seasoning; place
tomatoes on top and cover.
3. Cook very gently for 12–15
minutes, until the fish is soft. The
liquid must not be allowed to boil
during cooking – it should just
simmer very gently.

MEDITERRANEAN FISH KEBABS
Serves 4

A popular way of serving cod in
Greece.

1½–2lb (¾–1 kilo) cod
2 small onions
2 tablespoons cooking oil
4 tablespoons honey
3 tablespoons wine vinegar
1 tablespoon lemon juice
1 teaspoon dried mixed herbs
1 tablespoon finely chopped
parsley
garlic salt (optional)
pepper

1. Cut the cod into cubes.
2. Peel the onions, cut into
quarters and separate into pieces.
3. Thread the cod pieces on to
four skewers, alternating with
pieces of onion.
4. Place all the other ingredients
in a bowl and mix together.
5. Lay the skewers in a shallow
ovenproof dish (not metal) and
pour over the marinade.
6. Leave, covered, in a cool place
for 2 hours.
7. Cook under a moderate grill,
basting frequently with the
remains of the marinade.
8. Serve with boiled rice and a
salad.

COD WITH FRENCH MUSTARD SAUCE
Serves 4

Mustard sauce is a popular fish flavouring on the Continent.

1oz (25gm) butter
2 small onions, finely chopped
1 packet (14oz or 350gm) frozen cod steaks, thawed
juice of half a lemon
4 tablespoons dry white wine
1 level dessertspoon French mustard
salt and pepper
½oz (12gm) butter
1 level teaspoon chopped parsley

1. Preheat oven to moderate to moderately hot, 375 deg F or gas 5 (190 deg C).
2. Melt the 1oz (25gm) butter in a small pan. Fry onions until tender but not brown. Drain.
3. Lightly butter a shallow ovenproof dish.
4. Put the cod steaks in the dish, sprinkle with lemon juice.
5. Place a little of the onion on each cod steak.
6. Blend wine, mustard and seasoning together and pour over fish.
7. Cover, and cook in the centre of the oven for about 20–25 minutes.
8. When the fish is cooked, drain off liquor into a small saucepan.
9. Bring to the boil, and reduce by half.
10. Remove from the heat, and stir in the butter and parsley.
11. Pour over the fish and serve.

COD PALERMO
(Illustrated on page 53)
Serves 6

6 frozen or fresh cod steaks
2 medium onions
1 tablespoon salad oil
8oz (200gm) tomatoes
2 heaped tablespoons finely chopped parsley
salt and pepper
2 tablespoons Marsala

1. Preheat oven to moderate to moderately hot, 400 deg F gas 6 (200 deg C).
2. Arrange fish in a buttered ovenproof dish.
3. Chop onions finely and fry in the oil until pale golden.
4. Skin and chop tomatoes and add to pan of onions with all remaining ingredients, except Marsala.
5. Cover and simmer for 10 minutes.
6. Add Marsala. Spoon equal amounts over fish steaks then cook, uncovered, in centre of oven for 20 minutes.
7. Serve with freshly boiled long-grain rice or noodles.

SPANISH FISH WITH CHILLI AND TOMATO
Serves 6

6 cod or haddock fillets (about 2lb or 1 kilo)
2 medium onions
2 garlic cloves
2–4 red chillis
2 tablespoons olive oil
2oz (50gm) tomato purée
salt and pepper
1 teaspoon Tabasco sauce
½ pint (250ml) dry white wine

1. Clean and trim the fish.
2. Chop the onions, crush the garlic and tie the chillis in a piece of muslin.
3. Fry the onions and garlic in hot oil and when cooked add the tomato purée, chillis in the muslin, seasoning and Tabasco sauce.
4. Cook the fish in the tomato mixture with a little wine. When fish is tender discard the chillis in their bag and stir in the rest of the wine taking care not to break the fish and heat gently.
5. Season the sauce to taste and serve with the fish.

FISH WITH FENNEL
Serves 4–6

A very popular way of serving fish in France.

12 shallots
3oz (75gm) butter
1 tablespoon oil
1oz (25gm) flour
1 tablespoon tomato purée
2 large tomatoes, skinned and chopped
½ pint (250ml) cider or white wine
salt and pepper
¼ pint (125ml) milk or single cream
1–2 teaspoons chopped fresh fennel leaves or ½–1 teaspoon dried fennel
½ teaspoon grated lemon rind
1 whole sea bass, cod, haddock or carp (about 2½lb or 1¼ kilo)
12 tiny firm tomatoes

1. Preheat oven to moderate to moderately hot, 375 deg F or gas 5 (190 deg C).
2. Peel shallots and fry in half the butter and the oil a few minutes.
3. Stir in the flour and cook for 2–3 minutes.
4. Blend in tomato purée, tomatoes and cider or wine and cook until mixture begins to thicken; season well and add the milk or cream, but do not boil.
5. Add the chopped fennel and lemon rind.
6. Pour the sauce round the fish in an ovenproof dish, brush the fish with the remaining butter, melted, and cover with greased foil.
7. Cook for about 30 minutes in the centre of the oven, then add the small tomatoes. Remove the foil so as to brown the fish slightly and cook for a further 15 minutes.

SMOKED HADDOCK ENVELOPE
Serves 4

8oz (200gm) smoked haddock
5 tablespoons milk
½oz (12gm) margarine
½oz (12gm) flour
1 hard-boiled egg
2 teaspoons chopped parsley
seasoning
1 packet (7½oz or 187gm) frozen
puff pastry, thawed
milk to glaze

1. Preheat oven to hot, 425 deg F of gas 7 (220 deg C).
2. Poach the haddock in the milk for 10 minutes.
3. Drain off the liquor and make up to ¼ pint (125ml) with milk or water.
4. Make a thick white sauce with the margarine, flour and diluted fish liquor.
5. Flake the fish and chop the hard-boiled egg. Add to the sauce with the parsley and seasoning. Allow to cool.
6. Roll the pastry into a 10-inch square.
7. Spread the cooked filling diagonally across the centre.
8. Damp the edges of the pastry, fold the two opposite corners together, then fold the two remaining corners to the centre and seal the edges.
9. Place on a baking sheet, brush the top with milk and bake in the centre of the oven for 45 minutes, until brown and crisp.
10. Serve hot or cold.

HADDOCK WITH HORSERADISH SAUCE
Serves 4–6

A German way of serving haddock.

2½lb (1¼ kilo) haddock
fresh mixed herbs
salt and pepper
lemon juice
¼ pint (125ml) white vinegar
1oz (25gm) butter
1oz (25gm) flour
¼ pint (125ml) milk
1 tablespoon fresh or dried grated horseradish

1. Clean the fish and cut into portions and place in a pan with water to cover.
2. Add the herbs, salt and pepper, lemon juice and vinegar; simmer for about 15 minutes. Drain, reserving liquor.
3. Make a white sauce with the butter, flour, fish liquor and milk.
4. Cook, stirring, until thickened.
5. Add the horseradish and lemon juice. (If using dried horseradish blend it first with a little milk or cream, and season to taste.)
6. Arrange the fish on a heated serving dish and pour over the sauce.

HAKE ESPAGNOLE
Serves 4

1½lb (¾ kilo) hake fillets
4 tablespoons dried breadcrumbs
salt and pepper
1 tablespoon olive oil
1 onion, sliced
1 garlic clove, crushed
6oz (150gm) mushrooms, sliced
1 pimento, chopped
parsley
marjoram
¾ pint (375ml) tomato pulp
1 glass white wine
paprika pepper and chopped parsley to garnish

1. Preheat oven to very moderate, 325 deg F or gas 3 (170 deg C).
2. Cut the fillets into four and dust with some of the breadcrumbs. Place in an ovenproof dish and sprinkle with the remaining crumbs. Sprinkle liberally with salt and pepper.
3. Heat the oil in a pan and add the onion and garlic and cook very gently until soft but not coloured.
4. Add the mushrooms and chopped pimento, season, cover with a lid and simmer for 3 minutes.
5. Add a little chopped parsley and marjoram, the tomato pulp and white wine. Allow to simmer gently for 10 minutes.
6. Adjust the seasonings and pour over the fish.
7. Cover and bake in the centre of the oven for 50 minutes.
8. Serve garnished with a little paprika pepper and chopped parsley.

GERMAN FISH ROLLS IN PAPRIKA SAUCE
Serves 6

6 white fish fillets
½ lemon
1 onion
1 teaspoon herbs
1–2 teaspoons chopped parsley
2 teaspoons flour
2oz (50gm) margarine
¼ pint (125ml) top of the milk or single cream
1–2 teaspoons paprika pepper
pinch of sugar and salt
6 shallots

1. Wipe and trim the fish, sprinkle with grated lemon rind, chopped onion, herbs and parsley.
2. Roll the fish and secure with wooden cocktail sticks and then roll in flour.
3. Fry the rolls in the margarine for about 10 minutes.
4. Blend top of the milk or cream with paprika pepper, and a pinch of sugar and salt.
5. Pour over the fish in the pan and heat.
6. Fry the shallots and serve one on top of each fish roll.

SPANISH FISH STEW
Serves 4–6

2 tablespoons oil
1oz (25gm) butter
2 onions, finely chopped
1–2 garlic cloves, crushed
4 tomatoes
1 pint (approximately ½ litre) mussels
parsley
salt and pepper
1½lb (¾ kilo) mixed white fish
8oz (200gm) red mullet
(lobster tails, small crayfish and prawns can be used as available)
1 lemon
½ pint (250ml) white wine

1. Heat the oil and butter in a pan and stir in the onions and garlic. Add skinned and sliced tomatoes and continue cooking until soft.
2. Cook the mussels in water with parsley and seasoning until the mussels open.
3. Leave the mussels in their shells and chop the rest of the fish, removing shells, where necessary.
4. Add the white fish and red mullet to the tomato mixture with the lemon rind and juice, the wine and seasoning to taste.
5. Simmer until nearly tender then add the shellfish and heat through. Serve at once.

GERMAN LARDEN FISH
Serves 4

1 large or 2 small white fish
salt and white pepper
dried parsley
1 small onion, finely chopped
4oz (100gm) bacon
¼ tablespoon flour
1oz (25gm) fat or oil
1 small can tomato purée
pinch of sugar
pinch of ground cloves
2–3 tablespoons wine vinegar
browned almonds and diced green pepper to garnish

1. Clean the fish and sprinkle with salt, pepper, parsley and onion.
2. Trim bacon and cut into strips then wrap around the fish securing with wooden cocktail sticks. Dust with flour.
3. Fry gently in hot fat until cooked through. Place on a serving dish and keep warm.
4. Meanwhile simmer the tomato purée, sugar, cloves, vinegar and a pinch of salt in a saucepan for 10 minutes.
5. Serve the fish surrounded with the sauce and garnished with almonds and green pepper.

ITALIAN STUFFED FILLETS
Serves 4

8oz (200gm) cooked white fish
2oz (50gm) soft fine breadcrumbs
rind and juice of 1 lemon
1 tablespoon olive oil
1 tablespoon mixed herbs
4 large or 8 small white fish fillets
2oz (50gm) butter
3 tablespoons fish stock or white wine
seasoning

1. Preheat oven to moderate to moderately hot, 375 deg F or gas 5 (190 deg C).
2. Flake the cooked fish for the stuffing and add to breadcrumbs with lemon rind and juice, olive oil and herbs.
3. Roll each fillet around a spoonful of stuffing. Secure with wooden cocktail sticks and place in a well greased ovenproof dish.
4. Put a knob of butter on each and add the stock or white wine.
5. Cover and cook in the centre of the oven for 25–30 minutes.
6. Serve the fish with the cooking liquor spooned over.

SOLE AND SPINACH IN CHEESE SAUCE
Serves 6

In Holland this dish is called *westlandse tong.*

12 sole fillets
salt and pepper
juice of half a lemon
2½oz (62gm) butter
thinly pared lemon rind
½ bayleaf
3 peppercorns
parsley stalks
¾ pint (375ml) milk
1½oz (37gm) flour
2 egg yolks
8oz (200gm) Gouda cheese, grated
salt, pepper, nutmeg
1½lb (¾ kilo) mashed potato
1lb (½ kilo) cooked spinach

1. Preheat oven to moderate, 350 deg F or gas 4 (180 deg C).
2. Season each sole fillet with salt and pepper and sprinkle with lemon juice. Roll each fillet up neatly.
3. Put into a buttered ovenproof dish, dot with 1oz (25gm) butter, cover and bake in the centre of the oven for 15 minutes, until the fish is cooked.
4. Place on one side and reserve the fish stock. Increase the oven heat to hot, 425 deg F or gas 7 (220 deg C).
5. Add the lemon rind, bayleaf, peppercorns and parsley stalks to the milk and simmer gently for 10 minutes, then strain.
6. Make a sauce with remaining butter, the flour and flavoured milk. Stir in the fish stock and egg yolks (heat, but do not boil). Stir in most of the cheese and allow to melt.
7. Season well with salt, pepper and nutmeg.
8. Take an oval entrée dish and pipe or spoon a border of potato.
9. Spread the cooked spinach in the centre of the dish.
10. Place the sole fillets on top and coat with the sauce.
11. Sprinkle with remaining cheese and place in the oven for 20–30 minutes, to heat through and brown the top.

SOLE A LA CREME
Serves 4

A well-known sole dish from France.

4 sole fillets
salt and pepper
2 shallots
parsley sprigs
1 small bayleaf
3oz (75gm) butter
12 tablespoons white wine
1½oz (37gm) flour
2 egg yolks
½ pint (250ml) single cream
3 tablespoons double cream
1 tablespoon lemon juice
orange and lemon wedges to garnish

1. Preheat oven to moderate to moderately hot, 375 deg F or gas 5 (190 deg C).
2. Wipe fish and season well and put in a buttered ovenproof dish. The fillets may be rolled or folded into three. Add the chopped shallots, parsley sprigs and bayleaf. Dot with half the butter.
3. Pour over the wine and cover; cook in the centre of the oven until tender.
4. Make a roux for the sauce with the remaining butter and the flour. Stir fish liquor into it, cook, stirring, until thickened.
5. Whisk the egg yolks and add to the creams and lemon juice. Add to the sauce. Heat, but do not boil.
6. Season to taste. Arrange the fish on a heated serving dish.
7. Serve the fish coated with sauce and garnished with orange and lemon wedges.

BAKED SOLE WITH NORMANDY SAUCE
Serves 4

1 sole, filleted
1 tablespoon white wine
salt and pepper
8 mussels, cooked
8 button mushrooms, cooked
½ pint (250ml) fish stock (see method)
1½oz (37gm) butter
1oz (25gm) flour
1 egg yolk
juice of 1 lemon
salt and pepper

1. Preheat oven to moderate to moderately hot, 375 deg F or gas 5 (190 deg C).
2. Fold the fillets in two and place in a buttered dish.
3. Pour the wine over, season with salt and pepper and cook in the centre of the oven for 15–20 minutes, or until the fish is opaque.
4. Drain well, and keep the liquid; keep the fish warm.
5. Make ½ pint (250ml) fish stock from the fish and mussel liquid and add the mushroom trimmings.
6. Melt 1oz (25gm) of the butter, stir in the flour and cook for a few minutes.
7. Add the stock slowly, stirring until smooth.
8. Bring to the boil and cook for about 4 minutes, stirring.
9. Cool, add the egg yolk and reheat to thicken but do not boil.
10. Add the lemon juice and seasoning and whisk in the remaining butter.
11. Add the mussels and halved mushrooms and heat gently.
12. Serve fillets with sauce poured over.

FILLETS OF SOLE WITH CALVADOS
Serves 4

20–25 green grapes
4 tablespoons Calvados
2 soles (about 1lb or ½ kilo each)
½ pint (250ml) white wine
½ pint (250ml) water or cider
bouquet garni (bayleaf, thyme and parsley)
salt and pepper
4 tablespoons double cream
butter

1. With a sharp knife, skin and seed the grapes.
2. Soak them in the Calvados for 1 hour.
3. Fillet the sole and set aside.
4. Put the heads and backbones in a large saucepan with the wine, water or cider, bouquet garni, salt and pepper.
5. Bring to the boil and simmer for 15 minutes.
6. Strain the liquid into another saucepan and boil again.
7. Reduce to a gentle simmer and poach the fillets in this liquid for 5 minutes.
8. Remove the fish, drain, place on a serving dish and keep warm.
9. Raise the heat and reduce the liquid until it becomes thickened.
10. Gradually add the cream and butter, whisking.
11. Add the grapes and the Calvados. Heat without boiling, pour the sauce over the fillets and serve.

MACKEREL PROVENÇALE
Serves 4

Mackerel is often served this way in France.

4 mackerel
3 tablespoons lemon juice
3 tablespoons chopped parsley
1oz (25gm) butter
2 teaspoons French mustard
pinch of mixed herbs
olives and parsley to garnish

1. Preheat oven to moderate to moderately hot, 375 deg F or gas 5 (190 deg C).
2. Split mackerel and place them on a greased baking dish, flesh side up.
3. Sprinkle over lemon juice and chopped parsley.
4. Bake uncovered, in the centre of the oven, for 20 minutes.
5. Make mustard butter by mixing the softened butter with the French mustard and mixed herbs.
6. Form into pats and chill.
7. To serve, place a pat of butter on each fish and garnish with olives and parsley.

SARDINES MEDITERRANEAN STYLE
Serves 4

1½lb (¾ kilo) fresh sardines, sprats or smelts
little milk
1oz (25gm) flour
1–2 tablespoons chopped herbs (parsley, fennel or chervil)
oil for deep frying
lemon wedges to garnish

1. Clean the fish and remove the heads. Dip in milk and coat in a mixture of flour and herbs.
2. Fry the fish, a few at a time, in the heated oil for 2–3 seconds. Drain on absorbent paper and serve garnished with lemon wedges.

GERMAN CRAYFISH WITH SAUCE
Serves 4–6

8–12 crayfish
2 teaspoons salt
1 teaspoon vinegar
1 lettuce
chopped dill
bunch mustard and cress
1–2 teaspoons dry mustard
1 tablespoon sugar
1 teaspoon cayenne pepper
6 tablespoons olive oil
3 tablespoons white wine, malt vinegar or lemon juice

1. Wash the crayfish and put them into boiling water with half the salt and 1 teaspoon vinegar and cook for about 10 minutes.
2. Split the fish when they are cool and remove intestinal veins.
3. Shred the lettuce and add the dill and cress. Arrange in a bowl.
4. Blend the dry mustard, sugar, remaining salt, the pepper, olive oil and wine for the sauce.
5. Pile the fish piled on top of the salad and serve the sauce separately. (Alternatively, the sauce can be tossed with the salad.)

VALENCIA PAELLA
(Illustrated on page 53)
Serves 4

The famous Spanish rice, seafood and meat dish.

4 tablespoons oil
1 large onion, finely chopped
2 red peppers, diced
2 green peppers, diced
2 shallots, finely chopped
1 garlic clove, finely chopped
6oz (150gm) mushrooms, sliced
8oz (200gm) long-grain rice
pepper, salt and saffron
1 pint (approximately ½ litre) chicken stock
8–12oz (200–300gm) cooked chicken, diced
4oz (100gm) cooked prawns, peeled plus a few unpeeled prawns to garnish
1 large onion, cut in rings and fried

1. Heat the oil in a large pan.
2. Add the onion, peppers, shallots and garlic.
3. When the vegetables are soft, add the mushrooms and heat for 1–2 minutes.
4. Add the rice and cook for 1 minute, stirring continuously.
5. Add pepper, salt and a grain of saffron.
6. Add the stock gradually, bring to the boil; stir and lower the heat to simmer.
7. Cover and cook about 15 minutes, without removing lid or stirring.
8. Mix in the chicken, cover and cook for a further 5 minutes.
9. Add prawns and mix well. Adjust seasoning.
10. Turn into casserole dish or paella pan and garnish with previously fried onion rings, and whole, unpeeled prawns.

SHELLFISH PAELLA
Serves 8

2 medium onions
1 garlic clove
1 green or red pepper
4oz (100gm) margarine
1 small lobster
½ pint (250ml) prawns
1 pint (approximately ½ litre)
shrimps
1 packet (4oz or 100gm) frozen
scampi
12 green or black olives
12oz (300gm) long-grain rice
1½ pints (approximately ¾
litre) boiling water
¼ pint (125ml) white wine
(optional)
good pinch saffron
salt and pepper

1. Chop onions and garlic finely.
Cut pepper into strips.
2. Melt 1oz (25gm) of the
margarine in large pan, add
onions, garlic and green or red
pepper.
3. Add lobster, shelled and cut in
small pieces; prawns and shelled
shrimps, thawed scampi and
sliced olives.
4. Cook for 15 minutes until
onion is tender and scampi
cooked.
5. Remove and keep hot while
rice is cooking.
6. Melt remaining margarine in
pan, add rice and cook gently
until margarine is absorbed,
about 3–5 minutes, shaking the
pan occasionally.
7. Add boiling water and wine (if
used), or additional boiling water.
8. Add saffron, salt and pepper.
9. Cook until all liquid is
absorbed, then add fish etc.
10. Mix well and serve
immediately.

DUTCH MUSSELS
Serves 4

2 pints (approximately 1 litre)
mussels
1 onion, chopped
6 sticks celery, chopped
salt and pepper
8oz (200gm) tomatoes, skinned
and chopped
4oz (100gm) cheese, grated
lemon and parsley to garnish

1. Clean the mussels in cold
water and place in a pan with
onion, celery and salt. Cook until
all shells are open.
2. Remove the inside (discard the
black vein) and mix with pepper,
tomatoes and most of the cheese.
3. Put the filling back in the
shells, sprinkle with remaining
cheese and brown under a hot
grill.
4. Serve garnished with lemon
and parsley.

VIENNESE PRAWNS
Serves 4

8oz (200gm) peeled prawns
1oz (25gm) butter
4 tablespoons sherry or
Madeira
3 egg yolks
½ pint (250ml) milk
salt and cayenne pepper
8oz (200gm) boiled rice (raw
weight)
chopped chives or parsley and
a few whole prawns to garnish

1. Fry the prawns gently in
butter for 5 minutes.
2. Stir in the sherry or Madeira
and cook for 2–3 minutes.
3. Mix the egg yolks and milk
and pour on to the prawn
mixture.
4. Add the seasoning, and heat
very gently until thickened; do
not boil.
5. Spoon at once over the boiled
rice.
6. Serve garnished with chives or
parsley and a few whole prawns.

DUTCH SEAFOOD SPECIAL
Serves 4

8oz (200gm) sole
8oz (200gm) halibut
8oz (200gm) cod
6oz (150gm) butter
1 medium onion, diced
4oz (100gm) mushrooms, sliced
½ pint (250ml) shrimps
1 bayleaf
½ pint (250ml) white wine
3 egg yolks
juice of 1 lemon
tarragon and oregano
chopped parsley to garnish

1. Cut the white fish into small
pieces and cook with 4oz (100gm)
of the butter, the onion,
mushrooms, shrimps and bayleaf
in the wine for 10–15 minutes
until the wine is reduced to
one-third of its original quantity.
2. Drain off the juice and make it
up to ¼ pint (125ml), if necessary,
with more wine.
3. Whisk the egg yolks, lemon
juice and fish liquor in a basin
over a pan of hot water. Whisk
until the mixture thickens to a
cream. Whisk in the remaining
butter, a little at a time, off the
heat.
4. Add the tarragon and oregano
to season.
5. Mix the fish and sauce together
and serve garnished with chopped
parsley.

PORTUGUESE STYLE LOBSTER WITH BRANDY
Serves 4

A dish that is made the day before it is to be eaten.

6 pints (approximately 3 litres) water
10 medium onions, sliced
3 carrots, sliced
parsley and thyme
1 bayleaf
few peppercorns
salt and pepper
2 lobsters
3lb (1½ kilo) tomatoes, skinned
1 garlic clove, chopped
6oz (150gm) butter
½oz (12gm) flour
2 tablespoons brandy
scant ¼ pint (125ml) dry white wine

1. Place the water, onions, carrots, parsley, thyme, bayleaf, peppercorns and salt in a pan. Bring to the boil and simmer for 10 minutes. Strain into a clean pan and add the uncooked lobsters. (Reserve the onions.) Boil for 20 minutes, remove the lid and allow to cool.
2. Split and remove black intestinal line, the tail meat and roe. Cut the meat into about 10 pieces.
3. Mix the chopped tomatoes, cooked chopped onions, salt, pepper and garlic.
4. In another pan, mix the butter with the flour, add the tomato mixture and cook for 5 minutes.
5. Press through a sieve, or blend in a liquidizer, until smooth.
6. Place lobster on a baking dish, pour the sauce over it and add the brandy and wine.
7. Simmer for 8–10 minutes.
8. Remove from heat and keep until next day in the refrigerator.
9. An hour before serving, heat the lobster mixture in a double boiler and serve with boiled potatoes or rice.

CREAMED SCAMPI ITALIAN STYLE
Serves 3–4

1–2oz (25–50gm) butter
8oz (200gm) jumbo scampi
little flour
½ pint (250ml) single cream
salt and pepper
lemon juice
chopped parsley or chives to garnish

1. Melt half the butter in a frying pan or shallow fireproof dish.
2. Toss the scampi in flour and fry carefully. Add more butter if necessary and keep shaking the the pan. Take care not to overcook the scampi as they will toughen.
3. Pour in the cream, stir to make a sauce and cook for 1–2 minutes. Do not boil.
4. Season with salt and pepper and some lemon juice.
5. Sprinkle with chopped parsley or chives and serve at once.

PORTUGUESE SCAMPI
Serves 4

2 onions, chopped
1 small garlic clove, crushed
1 tablespoon oil
1lb (½ kilo) tomatoes, peeled and chopped
½ glass dry white wine
12 olives, stoned
salt and pepper
2oz (50gm) butter
12oz (300gm) long-grain rice
1½ pints (approximately ¾ litre) stock
1¼lb (600gm) scampi
oil

1. Make the sauce by frying half the onion and the garlic in oil for a few minutes.
2. Add tomatoes, wine, olives and seasoning.
3. Simmer gently over low heat for about 25 minutes.
4. Make the pilaff by heating butter in a large pan.
5. Add remaining onion and the rice and gently fry until golden brown, stirring all the time.
6. Add stock and season to taste.
7. Bring to the boil, stirring constantly.
8. Cover, and simmer very gently for 20 minutes. Arrange on a serving dish. Keep warm.
9. To serve, put scampi on skewers brush with oil and grill for 7–8 minutes.
10. Place scampi on top of pilaff on dish and serve the sauce separately.

LASAGNE WITH YOGURT TOPPING
(Illustrated on page 53)
Serves 4

Meat sauce:
½oz (12gm) lard
1 medium onion, chopped
1lb (½ kilo) lean minced beef
1 level teaspoon dried mixed herbs
1 can (15oz or 375gm) peeled tomatoes
2 level teaspoons cornflour
1 tablespoon Worcestershire sauce

Cheese sauce:
1oz (25gm) butter
1oz (25gm) flour
½ pint (250ml) milk
¼ level teaspoon dry mustard
1½oz (37gm) Cheddar cheese, grated
salt and pepper
6 sheets lasagne (about 4oz or 100gm)

Yogurt topping:
1 carton (5oz or 125gm) natural yogurt
1 egg
½oz (12gm) flour
1 tablespoon grated Parmesan cheese (optional)

1. Preheat oven to moderate to moderately hot, 375 deg F or gas 5 (190 deg C).
2. To make the sauce, melt lard in a pan and gently fry onion for 3 minutes, until soft.
3. Add beef, herbs and tomatoes and bring to the boil, stirring.
4. Simmer, uncovered for 30 minutes.
5. Mix cornflour with Worcestershire sauce and stir into the meat.
6. Return to boil for 1 minute, stirring.
7. To make cheese sauce, melt butter in a pan, stir in flour off the heat and blend in milk. Return to heat and bring to boil, stirring.
8. Remove from heat. Add mustard, cheese and seasoning.
9. Cook the pasta according to the directions or place in boiling salted water for 11 minutes; drain.
10. To make up the dish, arrange the meat, lasagne and cheese sauce in layers, in a 3-pint (approximately 1½-litre) ovenproof dish, finishing with a layer of lasagne.
11. To make topping, combine yogurt, egg and flour, mix well and spoon over lasagne. Bake in the centre of the oven for 20–25 minutes, until topping is set.
12. If liked, sprinkle with grated Parmesan cheese and brown under hot grill.

BOLOGNAISE SAUCE WITH SPAGHETTI
Serves 6

4 tablespoons vegetable oil
4oz (100gm) onions
1 carrot
1 stick celery
1 garlic clove
3oz (75gm) streaky bacon, diced
5oz (125gm) finely minced beef
5oz (125gm) tomato purée
1 can (8oz or 200gm) tomatoes
¼ pint (125ml) beef stock
1 bayleaf
pinch of nutmeg
black pepper
salt
12oz (300gm) spaghetti

1. Heat the oil and fry the chopped onion, carrot, celery and garlic until soft.
2. Stir in the minced beef and bacon and brown, stirring continuously.
3. Add remaining ingredients (except spaghetti) and season well.
4. Cover and simmer for 35–45 minutes.
5. Meanwhile cook the spaghetti in boiling salted water for about 10–12 minutes.
6. Drain and serve with the sauce and grated Parmesan cheese if wished.

SPAGHETTI NEAPOLITAN STYLE
Serves 6–8

1 tablespoon olive oil
2oz (50gm) ham or bacon fat, chopped
1 tablespoon chopped onion
pinch of pepper
1lb (½ kilo) tomatoes, peeled
1 tablespoon chopped basil
salt
1lb (½ kilo) spaghetti
4oz (100gm) Parmesan cheese, grated

1. Put olive oil, ham fat, onion and pepper in a saucepan and brown.
2. Add tomatoes, basil and a little salt.
3. Mix well and continue cooking gently for 15 minutes.
4. Cook the spaghetti in salted water until tender.
5. Drain and cover with the tomato sauce and half the Parmesan cheese.
6. Serve the remaining Parmesan cheese separately.

ITALIAN HAM AND PASTA SHELLS
(Illustrated on page 53)
Serves 4

1oz (25gm) butter
1 onion, chopped
1oz (25gm) flour
1 can (14oz or 350gm) tomatoes
2 tablespoons tomato purée
¼ pint (125ml) chicken stock
salt and pepper
pinch of sugar
bouquet garni
1 tablespoon chopped parsley
1 can (11oz or 275gm) ham, diced
6oz (150gm) pasta shells, cooked quickly in boiling salted water

1. Melt the butter and fry the onion lightly.
2. Stir in the flour, add all the remaining ingredients apart from the pasta.
3. Bring to the boil, stirring all the time, and simmer for a further 5 minutes.
4. Remove the bouquet garni, adjust the seasoning and serve on the drained pasta shells.

PIZZAS
Serves 6

A southern Italian dish.

**1lb (½ kilo) plain flour
2 level teaspoons salt
½oz (12gm) lard
about ¼ pint (125ml) water**

**Yeast liquid:
dissolve ½oz (12gm) fresh yeast
in ¼ pint (125ml) water or
dissolve 1 teaspoon sugar in
¼ pint (125ml) warm water and
sprinkle 2 level teaspoons dried
yeast on top. Stand for 10
minutes until frothy.**

**Filling:
1lb (½ kilo) strong Cheddar
cheese, grated
1lb (½ kilo) fresh tomatoes,
sliced or 1 can (15oz or 375gm)
tomatoes, drained
pepper
1 teaspoon basil or thyme**

**Topping:
anchovy fillets, capers, black
olives and onion rings**

1. Preheat oven to hot, 450 deg F
or gas 8 (230 deg C).
2. Mix flour and salt in a bowl
and rub in lard.
3. Add yeast liquid and sufficient
water to make a soft dough.
4. Knead dough until smooth,
firm and elastic and dough leaves
bowl clean.
5. Shape dough into a ball. Put
to rise in a large greased
polythene bag, loosely tied, or a
large greased pan with a lid, until
it doubles its size and springs
back when pressed with a lightly
floured finger. It will take 45–60
minutes in a warm place, 2 hours
at room temperature, 12 hours in
a cold room or larder, 24 hours in
a refrigerator.
6. Turn risen dough on to a
board and flatten with knuckles
or rolling pin into a long strip.
Brush with oil and roll up like a
Swiss roll. Repeat this three
times in all.
7. Divide dough into six pieces
and roll each piece to a flat circle
to fit six greased 6-inch (15-cm)
sandwich tins.
8. Brush dough with oil and
cover with alternate layers of
grated cheese, sliced tomatoes
and seasoning, finishing with a
layer of cheese.
9. Garnish as liked with anchovy
fillets, capers and black olives.
Onion rings can be added before
or after baking.
10. Bake for 20–30 minutes in the
centre of the oven.
(If you do not have six 6-inch
(15-cm) tins, press the dough into
six circles and bake on a flat
baking sheet. Or use four 7- or
8-inch (18- or 20-cm) tins if
available. Alternatively you can
make one large pizza by rolling
dough to fit a baking tray 12
inches (30cm) by 16 inches (40cm)
and bake for 35–40 minutes.)

RICE WITH PISTACHIO NUTS AND ALMONDS
Serves 4–6

From the eastern Mediterranean
where rice is often prepared this
way, if the dish is to form part of a
feast or a party menu. Saffron is
added partly because yellow is
the colour that is said to bring
happiness.

**1lb (½ kilo) long-grain rice
3oz (75gm) butter
¾ pint (375ml) water
¼–½ teaspoon powdered saffron
1oz (25gm) pistachio nuts,
blanched and coarsely chopped
1 tablespoon oil**

1. Soak the rice in boiling water
for 1 minute.
2. Drain and rinse well under
cold running water. Dry well.
3. Heat the butter in a large
saucepan and fry the rice until
it is transparent.
4. Add the water and saffron and
bring to the boil. Lower the heat
and cover tightly (this can be
done by placing a sheet of foil or
greaseproof between the top of
the pan and the lid).
5. Simmer for 15–20 minutes,
without stirring.
6. Meanwhile fry the nuts in the
oil until browned, then place in
a greased 1½–2-pint
(approximately ¾–1-litre) ring
mould. (This is the traditional
shape, but an 8-inch (20-cm) cake
tin could be used.)
7. Press the rice over the nuts
and keep hot for 4–5 minutes.
8. Turn on to a heated serving
dish and serve immediately.

POTATO LORRAINE

**1lb (½ kilo) boiled potatoes
4oz (100gm) cheese, grated
2–3 eggs
¼ pint (125ml) milk
salt and pepper
nutmeg
2oz (50gm) butter
1 hard-boiled egg, sliced**

1. Preheat oven to moderate to
moderately hot, 375 deg F
or gas 5 (190 deg C).
2. Slice the potatoes.
3. Sprinkle the bottom of a
greased pie dish with half the
cheese.
4. Cover evenly with the
potatoes.
5. Beat eggs, milk, salt and
pepper and nutmeg together.
6. Pour over potatoes, cover with
cheese and dot with butter.
7. Bake in the centre of the oven
for 30–35 minutes until custard is
set and browned.
8. Garnish with hard-boiled egg
slices.

SAVOURY POTATO TORTE
Serves 4–6

**2lb (1 kilo) sieved, cooked
potato
2oz (50gm) butter
4 tablespoons milk or cream
2oz (50gm) ham, diced
1 egg yolk
½ garlic clove
salt and pepper
2 egg whites
3oz (75gm) Camembert cheese,
cubed
dried breadcrumbs**

1. Preheat oven to moderate to
moderately hot, 400 deg F or gas 6
(200 deg C).
2. Beat together the potato,
melted butter and milk or cream.
3. Add the ham, egg yolk, crushed
garlic, salt and pepper to taste.
4. Whip egg whites stiffly and
fold in, alternately, with the
cheese.
5. Brush the inside of a cake tin
with a little butter and sprinkle
with breadcrumbs.
6. Spoon in the potato mixture
and bake in the centre of the oven
for 20–30 minutes.
7. Turn out the torte and serve
cut in wedges.

SAURE KARTOFFELN
Serves 4

A German dish; the name means 'sour potatoes'.

1½lb (¾ kilo) potatoes, peeled
4oz (100gm) lean bacon, de-rinded and chopped
1oz (25gm) butter
1oz (25gm) flour
½ pint (250ml) stock
salt and pepper
1 tablespoon white vinegar
1 teaspoon sugar
8oz (200gm) French beans, sliced

1. Boil potatoes until just cooked; cut into slices about a ¼ inch thick.
2. Fry bacon gently in butter.
3. Add the flour and cook gently without browning; add the stock gradually and bring to the boil.
4. Add the potatoes, salt, pepper vinegar, sugar and French beans.
5. Simmer for 30 minutes.

GOLDEN POTATOES
Serves 4–6

The traditional Danish way of cooking potatoes to serve with the Christmas Eve feast.

2 tablespoons granulated sugar
1oz (25gm) butter or margarine
2 cans (21oz or 525gm) new potatoes

1. Melt sugar in a frying pan, and when it is frothy and turning light brown, add the butter.
2. Put the potatoes in a colander, pour cold water over and shake them.
3. Toss potatoes in sugar and butter mixture in the frying pan.
4. Cook for 10 minutes over gentle heat until potatoes turn an even golden colour. Serve at once.

HEIDELBERG POTATOES
Serves 4–6

4 tablespoons cooking oil
½ teaspoon Tabasco sauce
1 large onion, sliced
1½lb (¾ kilo) potatoes, thinly sliced
1 level teaspoon salt

1. Put oil into a large frying pan, add Tabasco sauce, onion and potatoes.
2. Stir well, cover and fry gently.
3. Cook for about 20 minutes, stirring occasionally until the potatoes are tender and lightly browned.
4. Sprinkle with salt and serve.

ALGARVE BEANS
(Illustrated on page 54)
Serves 4–6

1 onion
4oz (100gm) salami
4oz (100gm) smoked ham or parma ham
1 tablespoon olive oil
1 pint (approximately ½ litre) chicken stock
1lb (½ kilo) broad beans
4oz (100gm) carrots
½ tablespoon tomato purée
seasoning

1. Preheat oven to cool, 275 deg F or gas 1 (140 deg C).
2. Finely chop onion, salami and smoked ham and fry in the olive oil for about 5 minutes.
3. Add chicken stock, beans, sliced carrots, tomato purée and seasoning.
4. Cover and cook in the centre of the oven for about 1 hour, until the beans and carrots are tender.
5. Serve with chunks of French bread.

ITALIAN STUFFED PEPPERS
Serves 4

These are eaten in many parts of the Continent mainly as a starter but they also make an unusual supper snack served with hot crusty bread.

4 medium peppers
2–3 tablespoons cooking oil
1oz (25gm) butter
1 small onion, finely chopped
2oz (50gm) mushrooms, sliced
4oz (100gm) long-grain rice
½ pint (250ml) chicken stock
3 tomatoes, skinned and chopped
2 level teaspoons made English mustard
1 tablespoon chopped parsley

1. Preheat the oven to moderate to moderately hot, 375 deg F or gas 5 (190 deg C).
2. Slice the top off each pepper and scoop out all the seeds and pith.
3. Cook in boiling, salted water for 5 minutes and then drain well.
4. Brush the outsides with a little oil and place in an ovenproof dish.
5. For the filling, heat the rest of the oil and the butter in a pan and fry the onion and mushrooms until soft.
6. Stir in the rice, cook over a gentle heat for 2–3 minutes and pour on the stock.
7. Cook, stirring occasionally, until most of the liquid has been absorbed.
8. Add the tomatoes, mustard and parsley and mix well.
9. Pile this mixture into the peppers, cover the dish lightly with foil and bake in the centre of the oven for 20 minutes.

DUTCH STUFFED PEPPERS
Serves 6

A variation, of the previous recipe, using meat and a cheese sauce.

6 green peppers
8oz (200gm) onions
2 garlic cloves
8oz (200gm) carrots
½ tablespoon oil
1lb (½ kilo) raw minced beef
salt and pepper
2oz (50gm) butter
2oz (50gm) flour
1 pint (approximately ½ litre) milk
pepper, salt and made mustard
4oz (100gm) Gouda cheese

1. Preheat oven to moderate to moderately hot, 375 deg F or gas 5 (190 deg C).
2. Cut the tops off peppers and scoop out seeds. Boil in salted water for 5 minutes. Remove carefully.
3. Chop onions, garlic and carrots then fry in oil with minced beef slowly for 20 minutes. Season well.
4. Fill the peppers with the mixture and place in an ovenproof dish.
5. Make the cheese sauce with the butter, flour, milk, seasoning and most of the cheese.
6. Pour the sauce around peppers. Sprinkle the remaining cheese on top and bake in the centre of the oven for 30 minutes, until peppers are tender.
6. Serve at once with boiled rice.

FRIED COURGETTES
Serves 4

4 courgettes
2 level tablespoons flour, seasoned with salt and pepper
1oz (25gm) butter
3 tablespoons salad oil

1. Wash courgettes well and cut into ½-inch thick rings.
2. Toss in flour, making sure both sides are well coated.
3. Heat butter and salad oil in large frying pan and add courgettes, a few pieces at a time.
4. Fry until golden on both sides.
5. Drain on absorbent paper, then transfer to a paper-lined serving dish.

AUBERGINE PARMIGIANA
Serves 4–6

A popular way of serving aubergines in Italy.

4 medium aubergines
salt and pepper
1 small onion, chopped
olive oil
1 can (1lb or ½ kilo) tomatoes, sieved
little finely minced cooked meat (optional)
6oz (150gm) Parmesan cheese, grated
2 eggs

1. Preheat oven to hot, 425 deg F or gas 7 (220 deg C).
2. Peel the aubergines and cut into long slices.
3. Sprinkle with salt and leave for 30 minutes.
4. Wash the slices and wrap in a cloth – squeeze well to remove all moisture.
5. Brown the onion in olive oil, then add the tomato pulp and cook for about 10 minutes.
6. Fry the aubergines in more oil and drain as soon as they are browned.
7. Put a layer of tomato sauce, in an ovenproof dish, followed by a layer of aubergine. Cover with more tomato sauce, the minced meat if used, and finally grated Parmesan cheese. Continue in these layers until the dish is full, finishing with a layer of cheese. (Reserve 2 oz (50gm) cheese.)
8. Beat the eggs with remaining Parmesan cheese and seasoning and pour on top.
9. Cook in the centre of the oven until golden brown.

STUFFED AUBERGINES
Serves 4

2 medium aubergines
½ teaspoon salt
2 teaspoons olive oil or melted butter
2oz (50gm) cooked bacon, diced
1 tablespoon chopped parsley
1 tablespoon finely chopped cooked onion
1 tomato, skinned and chopped
2oz (50gm) fresh breadcrumbs
2oz (50gm) Cheddar cheese, grated
½ pint (250ml) tomato sauce (see page 55)

1. Preheat oven to moderate to moderately hot, 375 deg F or gas 5 (190 deg C).
2. Wash the aubergines and remove the stalks, then cut in half lengthwise.
3. Cut round each half aubergine a ¼ inch from the skin and then criss-cross the surface lightly to ensure even cooking.
4. Sprinkle with salt and olive oil or melted butter.
5. Put in a greased ovenproof dish and cook in the centre of the oven for 15–20 minutes.
6. Mix together the bacon, parsley, onion, tomato and breadcrumbs.
7. Scoop out half the flesh from the centre of the aubergines, chop and mix it into the stuffing.
8. Fill the aubergine cases, mounding the stuffing, sprinkle with grated cheese and return to the oven for a further 15 minutes.
9. Serve hot with tomato sauce.

PISTO
Serves 4–6

4oz (100gm) butter
2 medium onions, chopped
1 garlic clove, crushed
1 level teaspoon chopped
parsley
1 small red pepper, sliced
1 small green pepper, sliced
8oz (200gm) courgettes, peeled
and sliced
4 large tomatoes, peeled and
sliced
8oz (200gm) cooked new
potatoes, diced
salt and pepper
4 eggs, beaten
4 slices fried bread

1. Melt 3oz (75gm) of the butter
in a large frying pan, add onions
and garlic and fry gently until
tender but not browned.
2. Add parsley, peppers,
courgettes and tomatoes. Mix
together and simmer for about 25
minutes, covered.
3. Meanwhile fry potatoes in
remaining butter until lightly
brown. Add to the vegetables,
cover and cook for a further 5
minutes.
4. Season and add the eggs. Cook,
stirring until lightly scrambled.
5. Spoon on to the slices of fried
bread and serve.

PETITS POIS A L'OIGNON
Serves 4

A French inspired way of making
a supper dish from eggs, cheese
and vegetables.

12oz (300gm) onions
2oz (50gm) butter
4oz (100gm) Gruyère cheese,
grated
2 eggs, beaten
salt and pepper
1 packet frozen petits pois,
thawed
1 pastry flan case (6 inches or
15cm), partly baked
grilled tomato slices to garnish

1. Preheat oven to moderate to
moderately hot, 400 deg F or gas 6
(200 deg C).
2. Slice onions, cook in butter
until soft.
3. Remove from heat, add 3oz
(75gm) of the cheese and the
beaten egg. Season and add peas.
4. Spread in flan case, sprinkle
with remaining cheese.
5. Cook in the centre of the oven
until the egg is set, about 15
minutes.
6. Garnish with grilled tomato
slices.

BROCCOLI POLONAISE
Serves 3–4

1 large packet frozen broccoli
2oz (50gm) butter or margarine
2oz (50gm) breadcrumbs
2 hard-boiled eggs, chopped

1. Cook broccoli in boiling salted
water. Drain.
2. Heat fat in pan and fry the
breadcrumbs until crisp.
3. Mix with chopped egg.
4. Arrange broccoli in a shallow
dish, cover with breadcrumb
mixture.
5. Serve at once.

BROCCOLI DANSK
Serves 4

1 packet frozen broccoli spears
6oz (150gm) streaky bacon,
de-rinded
2oz (50gm) cheese, grated

1. Preheat oven to moderate to
moderately hot, 400 deg F or gas 6
(200 deg C).
2. Cook broccoli in boiling salted
water. Drain.
3. Wrap rashers of bacon around
each broccoli spear and arrange
in an ovenproof serving dish.
4. Sprinkle with grated cheese
and cook in the centre of the
oven for 10 minutes, until bacon
is cooked and top browned.

BROCCOLI PARISIENNE
Serves 4–6

8oz (200gm) cooked chicken,
sliced
2 packets frozen broccoli
spears, cooked
1 can (4oz or 100gm) button
mushrooms
1 pint (approximately ½ litre)
white sauce (see Basic recipe,
page 100)
4oz (100gm) cheese, grated
salt and pepper
2 tablespoons cream
½ teaspoon Worcestershire
sauce

1. Place the sliced chicken in the
bottom of an ovenproof dish, lay
the broccoli on top, then add the
drained mushrooms.
2. Make the white sauce then stir
in 3oz (75gm) of the grated cheese,
season and add the remaining
ingredients.
3. Pour the sauce over the
broccoli, top with remaining
cheese and place under a
moderate grill for 5–10 minutes
until brown and bubbling.

POLISH BIGOS
Serves 4–6

1lb (½ kilo) Polish sauerkraut
salt and pepper
2 bayleaves
1lb (½ kilo) cabbage
2 dried mushrooms
6oz (150gm) lean pork, cubed
4oz (100gm) bacon, cubed
2 onions, chopped
½oz (12gm) lard
8oz (200gm) ham
4oz (100gm) Polish sausage
2oz (50gm) tomato purée

1. Pour small quantity of boiling water over sauerkraut, add bayleaves and boil until tender.
2. Slice the cabbage and cook in small quantity of boiling water until tender.
3. Soak the dried mushrooms in water, drain and boil until tender, cut in strips, then add them, together with pork and bacon to the sauerkraut and simmer for about 30 minutes.
6. Fry the onions in lard and add to the cabbage.
7. Mix the cabbage mixture with the sauerkraut mixture.
8. Cut the ham into strips, remove rind from sausage and slice.
9. Mix ham, sausage and tomato purée with cabbage and sauerkraut, season well and heat through. Serve.

DANISH SWEET SOUR RED CABBAGE
(Illustrated on page 54)
Serves 4–6

This dish can be prepared ahead and reheated. It can also be served cold.

1 medium red cabbage (about 3lb or 1½ kilo)
2 large cooking apples, peeled
1oz (50gm) butter
4oz (100gm) wine vinegar
1 tablespoon water
2oz (50gm) granulated sugar
pinch of powdered cloves
salt and ground black pepper
2 large tablespoons redcurrant jelly

1. Shred the cabbage and grate the apples.
2. Put them into a saucepan with the butter.
3. Cook, covered, over gentle heat until butter has melted.
4. Add the wine vinegar, water, sugar and cloves; continue cooking for 2 hours over gentle heat.
5. Season with salt and pepper; add the redcurrant jelly and cook for a further 15 minutes.

GERMAN SWEET AND SOUR CABBAGE
Serves 6

1 white cabbage (about 4lb or 2 kilo)
2oz (50gm) butter
2 level tablespoons honey
2 tablespoons lemon juice
¼ level teaspoon caraway seeds (optional)

1. Prepare and shred cabbage.
2. Cook in a little boiling salted water for 5 minutes, drain.
3. Melt butter and honey in a saucepan, add lemon juice, cabbage and caraway seeds.
4. Cook gently for about 10 minutes, until cabbage is just tender, stirring occasionally.

AUSTRIAN STUFFED CABBAGE LEAVES
Serves 4

1 onion, finely chopped
8oz (200gm) cooked meat, minced
2 level teaspoons German mustard
salt and pepper
2 tablespoons boiled rice
1 cabbage
stock
2 bayleaves
little cornflour (optional)
chopped parsley to garnish

1. Put the onion, meat and mustard in a bowl and mix well together.
2. Add 2 tablespoons cold water. Season well with salt and pepper and add the rice.
3. Carefully remove the leaves from the cabbage. Put in a pan of cold water, bring to the boil and simmer for 2 minutes. Drain well.
4. Remove any hard stalks on the leaves.
5. Put a spoonful of the meat mixture on each leaf and roll up neatly.
6. Arrange the rolls in a large pan and barely cover them with stock.
7. Add the bayleaves and simmer, covered, for 40 minutes.
8. Carefully lift out the cabbage rolls and place on a serving plate. Cover with either the stock, slightly thickened with cornflour, or with tomato sauce (see page 55).
9. Sprinkle generously with chopped parsley.

Old Danish rum pudding (see page 84) Hague's bluff (see page 85)

Italian torrone (see page 90) Boterletter (see page 93)

Spanish chocolate fried bread (see page 96)　　Smorrebrod or Danish open sandwiches (see page 97)

Nordic dip (see page 99)　　Polish New Year's Eve punch (see page 99)

SAUSAGE-STUFFED CABBAGE
Serves 6

Another Austrian way of preparing stuffed cabbage leaves.

1 green cabbage
1¼lb (600gm) pork sausagemeat
3oz (75gm) breadcrumbs
2 apples, peeled, cored and chopped
1oz (25gm) almonds, chopped
salt and pepper
1 egg, beaten
1 large can peeled tomatoes

1. Preheat oven to moderate to moderately hot, 375 deg F or gas 5 (190 deg C).
2. Remove the best leaves from the cabbage.
3. Cut away the firm stalk and blanch the leaves in boiling water.
3. Mix the sausagemeat, breadcrumbs, apple, almonds and seasoning, and bind with beaten egg.
4. Divide into six even-sized balls. Completely wrap each ball in a cabbage leaf, making a compact shape.
5. Place in an ovenproof dish, pour the tomatoes on top, and cook in the centre of the oven for 40–45 minutes.

RED CABBAGE
Serves 4

A very popular dish in Holland.

1lb (½ kilo) red cabbage
1lb (½ kilo) sour apples
¼ pint (125ml) water
2oz (50gm) sugar
1 teaspoon salt
4 cloves
4 tablespoons vinegar
2oz (50gm) butter

1. Trim and clean cabbage. Shred finely.
2. Peel, core and slice apples.
3. Place cabbage and apples in a pan, add the water, sugar, salt and cloves.
4. Cover and simmer gently until tender, about 45 minutes.
5. Remove cloves, add vinegar and butter.
6. Blend well over heat.
7. Adjust seasoning and serve hot with meat dishes.

DUTCH CURLY KALE AND POTATOES
Serves 4–6

2lb (1 kilo) kale
2lb (1 kilo) potatoes
6oz (150gm) streaky bacon
2oz (50gm) porridge oats
6 frankfurter sausages
salt and pepper

1. Clean kale, remove stalk and vein. Chop roughly.
2. Peel and cube potatoes. Cook kale together with the bacon in a little boiling salted water for 10 minutes. Add potatoes and porridge oats.
3. Place the frankfurters on the top of the mixture.
4. Cover with a lid and simmer for a further 30 minutes, until kale is tender and the potatoes quite soft.
5. Remove frankfurters and bacon and mash the potatoes and kale together. Season well.
7. Replace the sausages, and the bacon if liked and serve with mustard.

DANISH BROWN CABBAGE
Serves 4

Danish brown cabbage (*brunkaal*) is a traditional dish which should be served with sausages and a selection of cold meats and sausages of the pork variety. Mustard is also served with this dish.

2oz (50gm) granulated sugar
2oz (50gm) butter
3lb (1½ kilo) white cabbage, shredded
salt and pepper
2 tablespoons water

1. Brown the sugar in a heavy saucepan, taking care not to let it burn.
2. Add the butter and, when this has melted, tip in the shredded cabbage.
3. Toss the shredded cabbage, in the caramel mixture for 2–3 minutes, until well coated. Add the seasoning and water.
4. Cover saucepan with a lid. Continue to cook the cabbage over a low heat for a further 1–1½ hours, until tender.

NORWEGIAN CABBAGE
Serves 4

1½lb (¾ kilo) cabbage
1 carton soured cream
1 teaspoon caraway seeds
1 teaspoon salt
black pepper

1. Shred the cabbage coarsely and cook in boiling salted water for 8–10 minutes so that it is tender but still crisp.
2. Drain the cabbage well. Stir in the soured cream, caraway seeds, salt and pepper.
3. Toss lightly over a low heat until the mixture is thoroughly blended and the cream is heated through.
4. Serve with meat or bacon dishes, or serve cold as a salad.

RED CABBAGE IN CHIANTI CLASSICO
Serves 6

A Tuscan way of cooking cabbage.

4oz (100gm) onion, finely chopped
1oz (25gm) dripping
8oz (200gm) bacon, finely chopped
2½oz (62gm) flour
3lb (1½ kilo) red cabbage, thickly sliced
1 pint (approximately ½ litre) Chianti Classico

1. Preheat oven to moderate, 325 deg F or gas 3 (170 deg C).
2. Brown the onion in a large flameproof casserole in the dripping and bacon.
3. When golden brown, add the flour and cook until it turns golden brown.
4. Mix in the cabbage, cover and cook in the centre of the oven for about 30 minutes.
5. Add the Chianti Classico, stirring gently to mix the ingredients.
6. Cover and return to the oven and continue cooking for about another 1–1½ hours.

Desserts

There are some mouth-watering dessert recipes in this chapter, including delicious pancake ideas, exciting ways to serve the humble rice pudding and unusual ideas for serving apples and pears.

If we had a reputation with Mrs Beeton for prodigality in the 'take a dozen eggs' style of recipe, the Continent is equally egg-happy when making desserts. The Portuguese, in particular, like to use lots of eggs in making custard creams; the French, Italians and Russians use them in soufflé omelettes, zabaglione and sweet blintzes. Cheesecake is another popular dessert eaten in many central European countries. Apples are universally popular and appear in many ways in flans and apple cakes popular among northern European countries.

Continental people tend to serve fruits soaked in wines or liqueurs and accompanied by whipped cream and nuts. On the whole, apart from some dough and dumpling variations, puddings are not as heavy as ours though rice puddings do have more flavoursome variations. Further east, in Greece, the desserts become very sweet and heavy with honey. Some unusual flavours are sometimes added to dessert sweets – carrots and potatoes are used in some recipes.

DANISH MOLEHILLS
Serves 4

An easy-to-make sweet from Denmark, known as *muldvarpeskud*.

8oz (200gm) prunes, stoned and soaked
¼ pint (125ml) water
sugar to taste
lemon juice
½oz (12gm) blanched almonds
2 egg yolks
1½oz (37gm) icing sugar, sifted
1 tablespoon Madeira or sweet sherry
1 can (6oz or 150gm) cream, chilled
2oz (50gm) rye bread, grated
2oz (50gm) plain chocolate, grated

1. Cook the drained prunes with the water, sugar and lemon juice for 15 minutes over low heat.
2. Drain the prunes and when cold, place an almond inside each.
3. Arrange the prunes in a pyramid shape on a serving dish.
4. Beat the egg yolks with the icing sugar and add the wine.
5. Fold in the chilled cream and pour at once over the prunes.
6. Sprinkle the grated bread and chocolate over the top and serve at once.

SWISS APPLE FLAN
Serves 4–6

shortcrust pastry made with 8oz (200gm) flour (see Basic recipes, page 100)
8oz (200gm) cooking apples
4 tablespoons water
about 4oz (100gm) sugar
2 tablespoons apricot jam
2 red-skinned dessert apples

1. Preheat oven to moderate to moderately hot, 375 deg F or gas 5 (190 deg C).
2. Line a 6-inch (18-cm) flan ring with the pastry and bake blind in the centre of the oven for 25–30 minutes.
3. Wipe and pierce the cooking apples.
4. Place in an ovenproof dish with half the water and bake for about 30 minutes, until soft.
5. Remove the skins and sieve the flesh of the apples.
6. Add half the sugar, or sweeten to taste. Spread the purée in the cooked pastry case.
7. Heat the apricot jam, remaining sugar and water together until the jam has dissolved.
8. Boil rapidly until the glaze is thick and syrupy.
9. Wipe the dessert apples and leave the skin on.
10. Quarter and core the apples and cut into thin, even slices.
11. Arrange in an overlapping circle on the top of the flan.
12. Coat at once with the apricot glaze.

CHESTNUT AND APPLE CHARLOTTE
Serves 6–8

A delicious sweet from France.

7 slices white bread
juice of 1 orange
apricot jam
3oz (75gm) almonds, chopped
and toasted
1 medium can chestnut spread
or purée
sugar to taste
½ pint (250ml) apple purée
grated rind of half a lemon
¼ pint (125ml) double cream
¼ pint (125ml) evaporated or
creamy milk
¾oz (18gm) powdered gelatine
2 egg whites
apple wedges, dipped in lemon
juice and glacé cherries to
decorate

1. Remove crusts from bread and
cut five of the slices in half. Cut
the other two into triangles to fit
the base of a charlotte mould.
2. Sprinkle bread with orange
juice.
3. Spread one side of each slice
with apricot jam, and sprinkle
lightly with the nuts.
4. Line charlotte mould with
bread shapes, nut-side
downwards.
5. Sweeten chestnut spread to
taste and combine with apple
purée, lemon rind, cream and
evaporated milk.
6. Dissolve gelatine in a little
water and add to mixture.
7. When about to set, fold in
stiffly beaten egg whites.
8. Pour into lined mould. Chill to
set.
9. Unmould and decorate with
apple wedges and glacé cherries.

POLISH APPLE OR PLUM PIEROZKI
Serves 3–4

4oz (100gm) self-raising flour
pinch of salt
2 egg yolks
little cold water
8oz (200gm) cooking apples or
plums
soured or fresh cream or
custard

1. Sift flour and salt into a bowl,
make a well in centre and put in
egg yolks.
2. Mix in the flour from edges to
centre and add enough water to
make a fairly dry crumbly dough.
3. Form into a ball and knead
lightly until smooth enough to
roll.
4. Roll out thinly, cut into 2-inch
circles. Dampen edges.
5. Wash plums or peel, core and
slice apples into half-circle
slices.
6. Place fruit on pastry circles.
Fold over the fruit to make
semi-circular turnovers. (If liked,
the plum-filled pierozki can be
rolled into a dumpling shape.)
7. Seal edges tightly, pressing
with a fork on both sides of edges.
9. Have ready a large saucepan of
boiling salted water. Drop the
pierozki into the water, not too
many at a time, so that each has
plenty of room to cook.
9. When they rise to the top, they
are cooked. If plums are used,
turn down heat and cook for
about a further 10 minutes.
10. Drain and serve piping hot
with soured or fresh cream and
plenty of sugar as they are not
sweetened.

POLISH APPLE OR PLUM KNEDLE
Serves 4

A variation on the previous
recipe – this one has a potato
pastry.

3oz (75gm) self-raising flour
pinch of salt
3oz (75gm) mashed potato
1 egg
2–3 cooking apples or 8oz
(200gm) cooking plums
icing sugar to sprinkle

1. Mix flour, salt and mashed
potato to a firm dough with the
beaten egg.
2. Knead until smooth enough to
roll out, roll thinly and cut into
circles. Dampen edges.
3. Wash plums, or peel, core and
chop apples coarsely.
4. Place fruit in middle of pastry
circles, pinch up around fruit,
roll between the hands until
dumpling-shaped and dust with
flour.
5. Have ready a large saucepan
of boiling salted water. Drop
dumplings in; when they are done
they will rise to the top. If plums
are used turn down heat and cook
for about a further 10 minutes.
6. Drain well, sprinkle with icing
sugar and serve hot with
accompaniments as above.

SWEDISH APPLE CAKE
Serves 3–4

**2oz (50gm) soft white
breadcrumbs
1 level teaspoon cinnamon
1 level teaspoon grated lemon
rind
¼ level teaspoon salt
12oz (300gm) apple purée
4 tablespoons water
2 tablespoons lemon juice
10–12 drops liquid sweetener or
sugar to taste**

1. Preheat oven to moderate, 350
deg F or gas 4 (180 deg C).
2. Mix together breadcrumbs,
cinnamon, lemon rind and salt.
3. Grease a 1-pint (approximately
½-litre) dish.
4. Cover the bottom of dish with
half the breadcrumb mixture.
5. Spoon on the apple purée, then
add the remaining breadcrumbs.
6. Mix together the water, lemon
juice and sweetening. Sprinkle
this on top of the mixture.
7. Cook for approximately 45
minutes in the centre of the oven.
Serve hot.

BULGARIAN APPLE SUNDAES
Serves 4

**2 eating apples
1½oz (37gm) brown sugar
chopped nuts
½ pint (250ml) natural yogurt
4 maraschino or glacé cherries**

1. Wipe the unpeeled apples well
and grate coarsely.
2. Put into four individual
glasses, sprinkling on the sugar
and adding alternate layers of
chopped nuts and yogurt.
3. Decorate each with a cherry.

DUTCH APPLE TART
Serves 6

**shortcrust pastry made with
8oz (200gm) flour (see Basic
recipes, page 100)
1lb (½ kilo) apples, peeled and
cored
4oz (100gm) brown sugar
2oz (50gm) sultanas
1 level teaspoon cinnamon
rind of half a lemon
1 teaspoon icing sugar**

1. Preheat oven to hot, 425 deg F
or gas 7 (220 deg C).
2. Roll out the pastry and use to
line an 8-inch (20-cm) sandwich
tin. Trim the edges.
3. Roll out the trimmings and cut
into strips for the decoration.
4. Slice the apples and mix with
the sugar, sultanas, cinnamon
and grated lemon rind. Place this
mixture over the pastry and place
strips of pastry over the filling to
form the lattice.
5. Bake in the centre of the oven
for 10–15 minutes, then lower the
heat to moderate, 350 deg F or
gas 4 (180 deg C) and bake for a
further 30 minutes.
6. Sprinkle icing sugar over the
top and serve with cream.

FRENCH FLAMBE APPLES
Serves 4–5

**8–10 dessert apples
lemon juice
2 pints (approximately 1 litre)
water
8oz (200gm) brown sugar
1 teaspoon powdered cinnamon
6 tablespoons rum**

1. Peel the apples and cover with
cold water with lemon juice
added.
2. Measure the water into a
saucepan and add the sugar and
cinnamon and bring to the boil.
3. Drain the apples and place in
the water and simmer gently for
10–15 minutes, until the apples
are tender.
4. Remove the apples and place in
a serving dish; keep warm.
5. Boil the syrup until slightly
thickened. Pour over the apples.
Spoon over the rum and ignite.
Serve immediately.

CHESTNUT AND APPLE SURPRISE
Serves 6

**4 medium cooking apples
3 tablespoons water
sugar to taste
1 medium can chestnut purée
18 sponge finger biscuits
4 tablespoons Kirsch
½ pint (250ml) double cream
1oz (25gm) almonds, sliced
mint sprig**

1. Peel, core and slice the apples
and place in a saucepan.
2. Add the water and cook gently,
covered, until the apple is reduced
to a pulp. Sweeten to taste.
3. Sieve the pulp and allow to
cool.
4. Spread a little of the chestnut
purée in the base of a serving
dish.
5. Moisten the sponge fingers in
the Kirsch and arrange on the
base and around the sides of the
dish.
6. Cover the sponge fingers with
another layer of the chestnut
purée.
7. Spread the cooled apple purée
on top of this. Add another layer
of sponge fingers and top this
with the remaining chestnut
purée.
8. Whip the cream until almost
stiff and flavour with Kirsch.
Spread cream on top.
9. Decorate with almonds, and a
mint sprig in the centre.
10. Chill before serving.

TARTE AUX POMMES JOSEPHINE
Serves 6

A French-style recipe from Frederick's restaurant in London.

rich shortcrust pastry made
with 6oz (150gm) flour (see
Basic recipes, page 100)
1½lb (¾ kilo) cooking apples
8oz (200gm) granulated sugar
2 tablespoons water
apricot jam
2–3 peaches or cherries to
decorate

1. Preheat oven to moderate, 350
deg F or gas 4 (180 deg C).
2. Line an 8-inch (20-cm) buttered
flan case with pastry and bake
blind in the centre of the oven for
25–30 minutes. Cool.
3. Peel, core and slice the apples
and leave in water and lemon
juice.
4. Put the sugar and water in a
heavy pan over low heat to
caramelize.
5. Shake the pan occasionally but
do not stir. When the caramel is a
rich golden colour, dry the apples
well and carefully add to the
caramel.
6. Cook for about 5 minutes or
until apples are soft but not
pulped, turning them frequently
with a wooden spoon. Leave to
cool.
7. Brush the flan case with some
melted apricot jam.
8. Spoon in the apples and a
little of the caramel.
9. Arrange the sliced peaches or
cherries decoratively on top.
10. Reheat the remaining caramel
and let it cook until it becomes
darker in colour.
11. Pour it carefully over the
filling and allow to cool before
serving.

ITALIAN APPLE FRITTERS
Serves 4

4oz (100gm) plain flour
large pinch of salt
1 egg
¼ pint (125ml) milk
3–4 cooking apples
lemon juice
caster sugar
little brandy or rum
2oz (50gm) butter and 3
tablespoons oil for frying

1. Prepare a coating batter using
the flour, salt, egg and milk.
2. Peel and core the apples and
cut into thin slices.
3. Rub each slice with lemon
juice, sprinkle with sugar and
leave to soak for 30 minutes in
brandy or rum.
4. Dip each slice in the batter and
fry for about 2 minutes.
5. Drain and sprinkle with sugar.
Serve hot.

SCANDINAVIAN PUDDING
Serves 4

1oz (25gm) margarine
2lb (1 kilo) cooking apples,
peeled, cored and sliced
2oz (50gm) caster sugar
2 tablespoons water
squeeze of lemon juice
¼ level teaspoon cinnamon
2oz (50gm) margarine
2oz (50gm) cornflakes
2oz (50gm) soft brown sugar
¼ pint (125ml) double cream

1. Place the first seven
ingredients in a saucepan and
cook gently until soft. Sieve to
make a purée.
2. Melt margarine, remove pan
from heat and stir in cornflakes
and sugar.
3. Place half the apple purée in
the bottom of a glass dish, cover
with half the cornflake mixture
and then spread over the lightly
whipped cream.
4. Spread remaining apple over
cream, and finally the remaining
cornflake mixture.
5. Chill thoroughly before
serving.

APFELKUCHEN
Serves 6–8

A favourite German sweet.

6oz (150gm) margarine
6oz (150gm) plain flour, sieved
1 tablespoon water
1 level tablespoon caster sugar
1 heaped tablespoon rolled oats
1lb (½ kilo) cooking apples,
peeled, cored and sliced
2 eggs, separated
2oz (50gm) caster sugar
½oz (12gm) ground almonds
2oz (50gm) almonds, chopped
1 tablespoon cream or top of
the milk
chopped almonds to decorate

1. Preheat oven to moderate to
moderately hot, 375 deg F or gas 5
(190 deg C).
2. Place 4oz (100gm) of the
margarine, 2 tablespoons of the
flour and the water in a mixing
bowl.
3. Cream with a fork for about ½
minute, until well mixed.
4. Stir in the remaining flour and
the tablespoon sugar to form a
fairly soft dough. Knead lightly.
5. Roll out fairly thinly and line
an 8-inch (20-cm) fluted flan ring
placed on a baking sheet.
6. Sprinkle over the rolled oats
and arrange the apple slices in
the flan ring.
7. Mix together the remaining
margarine, the egg yolks, ground
almonds, chopped almonds and
cream or top of the milk.
9. Fold in the stiffly whisked egg
whites and spoon the mixture
over the apples.
10. Decorate with chopped
almonds.
11. Bake in the centre of the oven
for 25 minutes.
12. Remove the flan ring carefully
and return the flan to the oven for
a further 10–20 minutes, until the
flan is cooked and the filling has
set.
13. Serve hot or cold, with cream
or custard.

APPLE STRUDELS
Serves 4–6

Austria's famous pastry and apple creation.

⅛oz (6gm) fresh yeast
1 teaspoon sugar
4 tablespoons milk
12oz (300gm) flour
pinch of salt
4oz (100gm) butter
extra milk to mix
2 tablespoons breadcrumbs
1¼lb (600gm) apples, peeled,
cored and thinly sliced
pinch of spice
3oz (75gm) sugar
2–4oz (50–100gm) sultanas
2oz (50gm) almonds, chopped
little melted butter
icing sugar to sprinkle

1. Preheat oven to hot, 425 deg F or gas 7 (220 deg C).
2. Cream the yeast with the 1 teaspoon sugar and the warmed milk.
3. Put into a warm place for about 15 minutes.
4. Sieve the flour and salt into a warm basin, rub in half the butter and add the yeast liquid and enough tepid milk to make a firm dough. Knead lightly.
5. Cover with cloth, leave in a warm place for 30 minutes.
6. Spread a clean teatowel on the table, flour lightly, then roll and pull the dough with your fingers until it is so thin you can see the colours of the cloth beneath.
7. Fry the breadcrumbs in the remaining butter. Cool slightly and sprinkle over the stretched dough. Mix together the apples, spice, sugar, sultanas and almonds and arrange over the breadcrumbs.
8. Roll up the dough, like a Swiss roll, to enclose the filling.
9. Lift on to a greased baking sheet and brush with a little melted butter.
10. Allow to prove in a warm place for 20 minutes. Bake in the centre of the oven for about 20 minutes, then lower the heat to moderate, 350 deg F or gas 4 (180 deg C) and cook for a further 15–20 minutes.
11. Serve hot or cold sprinkled with icing sugar.

LIMBURG CHERRY FLAN
Serves 8

The flans made in Limburg are famous all over Holland.

6oz (150gm) plain flour
4oz (100gm) unsalted butter
2oz (50gm) caster sugar
1 egg yolk
1 can Morello cherries
1 heaped teaspoon arrowroot
¼ pint (125ml) cherry juice
½ pint (250ml) double cream

1. Preheat oven to moderate to moderately hot, 375 deg F or gas 5 (190 deg C).
2. Make a pastry using the flour, butter and sugar and egg yolk. Press into a well-buttered 10-inch (25-cm) flan tin. Prick the bottom with a fork.
3. Bake blind in the centre of the oven for 30 minutes. Cool slightly then remove from the tin.
4. Drain and stone cherries and place on pastry base.
5. Make a glaze by blending the arrowroot with the cherry juice; stir over a low heat until the mixture thickens.
6. Allow to cool slightly, then spoon over the cherries.
7. Decorate with freshly whipped cream.

DUTCH PLUM TART
Serves 4

6oz (150gm) butter
2oz (50gm) caster sugar
2oz (50gm) ground almonds
grated rind of 1 lemon
8oz (200gm) plain flour
½ teaspoon cinnamon
1½lb (¾ kilo) plums, cooked and
sweetened
icing sugar to sprinkle
jam to glaze

1. Preheat oven to moderate to moderately hot, 375 deg F or gas 5 (190 deg C).
2. Place butter, sugar, ground almonds and lemon rind in a basin with 2 tablespoons of the flour.
3. Beat together until soft and add remaining flour and the cinnamon. Mix to a soft dough.
4. Knead lightly and roll out two-thirds of the dough. Use to line an 8-inch (20-cm) fluted flan ring. Prick base with a fork.
5. Chill for 30 minutes.
6. Fill flan with drained plums and make a lattice work with the remaining dough. Bake in the centre of the oven for 30–35 minutes.
7. Sprinkle lattice work with icing sugar and brush plums with a little melted jam.
8. Serve with cream or custard.

STRAWBERRIES ITALIAN STYLE
Serves 4–6

1lb (½ kilo) strawberries
1 pint (approximately ½ litre)
sweet white wine
4oz (100gm) sugar
¾ pint (375ml) double cream,
whipped

1. Hull the strawberries and soak them in the wine.
2. Drain and place in a serving bowl. Cover with the sugar and whipped cream.
3. Place in refrigerator for 2 hours before serving.

MELON COPENHAGEN
(Illustrated on page 54)
Serves 6

4oz (100gm) long-grain rice
½ pint (250ml) water
½ teaspoon salt
1 melon
1 small can fruit cocktail
1 banana, peeled and sliced
12 grapes, black and green
1 orange, skinned and diced
½ lemon
Maraschino, Cognac or apricot
brandy
½ pint (250ml) double cream
2½ tablespoons sugar
few drops vanilla essence
fresh fruit to decorate

1. Put rice, water and salt into a
saucepan.
2. Bring to the boil and stir once.
Lower heat to simmer.
3. Cover and cook for 15 minutes,
or until rice is tender and liquid
absorbed. Leave to cool.
4. Cut off the top of the melon
and remove the seeds.
5. Hollow out the melon and cut
the flesh into bite-size pieces.
6. Sprinkle with Maraschino and
chill until ready to serve.
7. Drain the fruit cocktail, mix
with banana, grapes, orange,
melon and rice.
8. Add a little lemon juice, grated
lemon rind and a touch of
Maraschino. Chill until ready to
serve.
9. Whip the cream, add sugar and
vanilla essence.
10. Fold gently into fruit mixture.
Spoon into the hollowed-out
melon. Serve decorated with fresh
fruit as available.

YOGURT AND FRUIT
Serves 4

Yogurt and fruit is a popular
sweet in Holland.

1 can (7½oz or 187gm)
raspberries
½oz (12gm) gelatine
2½oz (62gm) caster sugar
(optional)
1 pint (approximately ½ litre)
yogurt
juice of 1 lemon
¼ pint (125ml) double cream

1. Drain raspberries.
2. Heat the fruit juice and
gelatine gently until all the
gelatine is dissolved. Add sugar
if used. Allow mixture to cool.
3. Blend the mixture with the
yogurt and lemon juice, fold in
raspberries.
4. Pour into individual glass
sundae dishes or into an oiled
1½-pint (approximately ¾-litre)
mould. Leave to set.
5. Serve decorated with whipped
cream; serve sponge finger
biscuits separately. (If a mould is
used, turn the mixture on to a
serving dish.)

PEARS PORTUGUESE
Serves 4

2 large pears, peeled and
halved
¼ pint (125ml) water
¼ pint (125ml) single cream
1 packet raspberry jelly,
dissolved in 1 pint
(approximately ½ litre) water
½oz (12gm) gelatine
¼ pint (125ml) double cream
chopped walnuts, angelica and
glacé cherries to decorate

1. Simmer the halved pears in the
water until tender. Place on a
cake rack to drain and cool.
2. Mix the single cream with ¼
pint (125ml) of the cooled jelly.
3. Dissolve the gelatine in
another ¼ pint (125ml) of the jelly
and add this to the cream mixture.
5. Chill until a coating
consistency. Arrange the pears in
a serving dish, pour over the jelly
mixture and allow to set.
6. Coat the pears with the
remaining jelly and leave to set.
Pipe swirls of whipped cream
around the edges and decorate
with chopped walnuts, angelica
and glacé cherries.

FRENCH PEAR GATEAU
Serves 8

6oz (150gm) margarine
6oz (150gm) sugar
2 eggs
8oz (200gm) self-raising flour,
sieved
1 dessertspoon grated orange
rind
1 dessertspoon grated lemon
rind
4oz (100gm) chopped mixed
peel
milk to mix
apricot jam
3oz (75gm) nuts, chopped and
toasted
2–3 ripe pears, peeled, cored
and halved
glacé cherries to decorate

1. Preheat oven to moderate, 350
deg F or gas 4 (180 deg C).
2. Cream margarine and sugar
until light and fluffy. Gradually
beat in the eggs. Fold in sieved
flour, grated rinds and chopped
peel and mix to a soft consistency
with a little milk.
3. Place mixture in a greased and
lined 2-lb (1-kilo) loaf tin. Bake in
the centre of the oven for
approximately 1 hour. Turn out
and cool on a wire tray.
4. Spread sides of cake with
apricot jam and coat with
chopped toasted nuts.
5. Arrange pear halves on top of
cake and glaze with melted,
sieved apricot jam. Decorate with
glacé cherries.

FRENCH PEAR SAVARIN
Serves 8

8oz (200gm) plain flour
scant ½oz (12gm) fresh yeast
3 tablespoons warm milk
4 eggs
6oz (150gm) butter
½ teaspoon salt
½oz (12gm) sugar
1 pear, peeled, cored and
chopped
6 tablespoons water
4 tablespoons sugar
1 tablespoon rum
6oz (150gm) apricot jam,
warmed and sieved
4 ripe pears, peeled, cored and
halved
juice of 1 lemon

1. Preheat oven to moderate to
moderately hot, 400 deg F or gas 6
(200 deg C).
2. Sieve flour into a warmed bowl.
3. Make a well in the centre and
add the yeast, blended with the
milk and eggs. Mix by hand for a
few minutes, until evenly blended.
4. Dot the surface with small
pieces of softened butter.
5. Cover the bowl and put in a
warm place until mixture doubles
in size.
6. Add salt and ½oz (12gm) sugar
and beat thoroughly, until
mixture begins to stiffen,
approximately 5–8 minutes.
(Alternatively, use the dough
hook of an electric mixer.)
7. Stir in chopped pear.
8. Place mixture into a large
greased savarin mould – the
mould should not be more than
half full. Leave to prove until
mixture is level with top of the
mould.
9. Bake in the centre of the oven
for 10 minutes and then reduce
heat to moderate, 350 deg F or
gas 4 (180 deg C), and cook for a
further 20–25 minutes.
10. Meanwhile dissolve water,
sugar and rum in a small
saucepan, bring to the boil and
simmer to form a light syrup.
11. Unmould savarin whilst hot
and immediately spoon over the
warm syrup.
12. When cool, spoon over half
the apricot jam.
13. Brush pear halves with lemon
juice, and coat with remaining
apricot jam. Serve with the
savarin.

BRANDIED PEARS
Serves 6

A delicious sweet from France.

6 conference pears
3 level tablespoons caster
sugar
3 tablespoons water
6 level tablespoons honey
2 tablespoons brandy

1. Peel the pears but leave whole.
2. Put the sugar and water in a
pan and gently heat the mixture,
stirring frequently, until the
sugar has dissolved.
3. Stir in the honey, add the pears
and poach over a low heat until
tender. (Do not let them go
mushy – they must retain their
shape.)
4. Allow to cool in the syrup,
spooning it over occasionally.
5. Stir in the brandy and chill.
6. Serve the pears in a shallow
dish with the syrup poured
around. Serve with a bowl of
whipped cream.

PEAR IMPERATRICE
Serves 4–6

1 can (1lb 13oz or 725gm) pear
halves, drained
8 maraschino cherries
2 cans (1lb or ½ kilo) creamed
rice
grated rind of 1 lemon
3 tablespoons maraschino juice
chocolate curls to decorate

1. Arrange the pear halves
around the side of a glass dish;
place a maraschino cherry in the
centre of each.
2. Blend the creamed rice, lemon
and maraschino juice together
and spoon into the centre.
3. Decorate the top with
chocolate curls and serve.

FRUIT COMPOTE
Serves 6

12oz (300gm) sugar
1 pint (approximately ½ litre)
water
juice of 1 lemon
6 pears, peeled, cored and
halved
4oz (100gm) dried or glacé
apricots (if dried soak
overnight)
4oz (100gm) dates, stoned
orange food colouring

1. Dissolve the sugar in water
and boil until syrupy.
2. Add the lemon juice and fruits,
except the dates, and simmer for
15–20 minutes.
3. Remove fruits to a large bowl.
4. Tint the syrup with a few drops
of orange food colouring, and
pour over the fruits and chill.
5. Decorate with stoned dates. (In
winter the compote may be served
hot.)

COEUR A LA CREME
Serves 6

A superb French sweet,
traditionally served in perforated
heart-shaped moulds, with
summer fruits such as
strawberries, raspberries, peaches
or blackcurrant purée.

8oz (200gm) cottage cheese
½ pint (250ml) double cream
2 level tablespoons icing sugar
8oz (200gm) strawberries,
hulled
1 teaspoon lemon juice
2 tablespoons caster sugar

1. Rub cottage cheese through
sieve into mixing bowl.
2. Stir in the double cream and
icing sugar and beat well.
3. Press into six individual *coeur
à la crème* moulds (cottage cheese
cartons, lined with muslin and
punched with holes, are good
substitutes for the traditional
dishes) and leave overnight in the
refrigerator or cool place.
Alternatively, place cheese
mixture in a muslin-lined sieve
and allow to drain.
4. Unmould and arrange on a
serving dish with fresh
strawberries which have been
sprinkled with lemon juice and
caster sugar.
5. Serve with a jug of single
cream and with almond biscuits.

SCANDINAVIAN FRUIT PUDDING
Serves 4–6

1lb (½ kilo) rhubarb
2oz (50gm) sugar
1 packet frozen raspberries, thawed
1 level tablespoon arrowroot

1. Cook the rhubarb with the sugar over a low heat until soft and pulpy.
2. Purée the raspberries through a sieve and mix with the cooked rhubarb.
3. Blend the arrowroot with a little cold water, mix in a little of the warm mixture, then return to the pan and heat gently stirring all the time, until the mixture thickens.
4. Pour into sundae glasses and serve chilled, with cream.

ITALIAN STRAWBERRY TORTONI
Serves 4

1oz (25gm) caster sugar
8oz (200gm) frozen strawberries, just thawed
¼ pint (125ml) double cream
1 egg white, stiffly beaten
1 teaspoon lemon juice or Kirsch
3 macaroons, coarsely crushed

1. Mix together the sugar and juice from the strawberries.
2. Whip the cream until thickened and fold in the beaten egg white.
3. Fold in the lemon juice or Kirsch, the sugar syrup from the strawberries and finally the crushed macaroons.
4. Divide between four sundae glasses and stud the top with the whole strawberries. Serve immediately.

CHESTNUT SUPREME
Serves 4

A delicious sweet from France.

4oz (100gm) cooking chocolate
2 tablespoons strong black coffee
1 tablespoon clear honey
2½oz (62gm) unsalted butter
1lb (½ kilo) chestnut purée
3oz (75gm) currants
langue de chat biscuits or sponge finger biscuits

1. Line a 5-inch (13-cm) mould with foil.
2. Place the chocolate, coffee and honey in a bowl over hot water and stir until melted.
3. Stir in the butter.
4. Add the chocolate mixture to the chestnut purée and beat well together.
5. Add the currants.
6. Put a layer of the mixture (about 1 inch thick) in the bottom of the mould and leave to set in a cool place.
7. Arrange the langue de chat or sponge finger biscuits around the sides of the mould and fill with the rest of the mixture.
8. Cover with foil and chill. Unmould to serve.

ITALIAN STUFFED BAKED ORANGES
(Illustrated on page 54)
Serves 4

A medieval dessert that was first served in Venice 400 years ago.

4 oranges
4–6 dates
few almonds or walnuts, chopped
3 tablespoons clear honey
2 tablespoons caster sugar
juice of 1 small lemon

1. Preheat oven to moderate to moderately hot, 375 deg F or gas 5 (190 deg C).
2. Peel oranges removing all pith. Place the oranges in a pan with some of the rind, cover with hot water and simmer for 30 minutes.
3. Remove from the water, save the liquid and cool. Core a deep hole in each orange.
4. Stone the dates.
5. Chop into small pieces and mix with almonds or walnuts, or a mixture of both.
6. Fill the orange holes with the date mixture and place in an ovenproof dish.
7. Boil ¾ pint (375ml) of the orange water, the honey and sugar together for 2–3 minutes.
8. Add lemon juice and pour over the oranges.
9. Bake for 1 hour, spooning over the syrup occasionally.
10. Cool and chill. Serve very cold. (This can be turned into a spectacular dessert by placing a sugar cube, which has been dipped in brandy, on each orange and igniting them at table.)

ORANGE PUDDING
Serves 4–6

A typical sweet custard dessert from Portugal.

10oz (250gm) sugar
6 eggs
juice of 1½ oranges
grated rind of 2 oranges
butter
caster sugar
whipped cream and fresh orange segments to decorate

1. Preheat oven to moderate to moderately hot, 375 deg F or gas 5 (190 deg C).
2. Beat the sugar, eggs, orange juice and rind together.
3. Grease an ovenproof mould with butter and coat with caster sugar. Spoon in the mixture.
4. Bake in the centre of the oven for 45 minutes–1 hour. Test to see if cooked, with a toothpick which should come out clean. Allow to cool.
5. Turn out of mould on to a plate and decorate with whipped cream and fresh orange segments.

NATILLAS
Serves 4

A traditional Spanish dessert.

**1 pint (approximately ½ litre)
milk
powdered vanilla or few drops
vanilla essence
5 egg yolks
6oz (150gm) sugar
1oz (25gm) maize flour
lemon or orange slices to
decorate**

1. Boil the milk with the vanilla.
2. Place the yolks, sugar and
flour in a saucepan; mix them
together then add the milk.
3. Put the saucepan on a low
heat and stir, with a wooden
spoon, until the mixture starts to
thicken, without letting it boil.
4. When cooked, pour in a dish
and leave to cool.
5. Serve decorated with lemon or
orange slices. If liked, serve with
whipped cream and sponge finger
biscuits.

ZABAGLIONE
Serves 4

This Sicilian dish is traditionally
served at wedding feasts 'for
strength'. It is made by whisking
the egg yolks, sugar and Marsala
together over a constantly low
heat.

**4 egg yolks
4oz (100gm) icing sugar
¾ wine glass Marsala**

1. Mix egg yolks and sugar with
1 teaspoon water in the heated
pan.
2. When the mixture is smooth,
add the Marsala a little at a time,
whisking well.
3. Continue to whisk and heat
gently until the mixture is soft,
foamy and velvety. (Alternatively,
the mixture can be whisked in a
bowl placed over a pan of hot
water, but this does take longer.)
4. Pour into glasses and serve
immediately.

CARAMEL CUSTARD
Serves 4

A typical recipe from Portugal.
Called '365' because of the number
of days on which restaurants
seem to serve it.

**3oz (75gm) granulated sugar
2 whole eggs
2 yolks
2oz (50gm) caster sugar
vanilla essence
1 pint (approximately ½ litre)
milk**

1. Preheat oven to moderate, 350
deg F or gas 4 (180 deg C).
2. Put the granulated sugar into
a strong saucepan and allow it to
melt slowly without stirring.
When beginning to colour, stir
occasionally until a good brown
colour.
3. Pour into a warmed soufflé
dish or ovenproof dish and turn
the dish to coat the bottom and
sides.
4. Break the eggs into a basin,
add the caster sugar and vanilla
essence and whisk with a fork.
5. Scald the milk and pour over
the eggs, stirring well, and then
pour into the soufflé dish. Cover
with paper.
6. Stand the dish in a tin
containing hot water and cook in
the centre of the oven for 45–50
minutes.
7. Remove and leave to cool,
before turning out on to a deep
dish to allow room for the
caramel.

DUTCH PANCAKES WITH SYRUP
Makes 6

The Dutch love pancakes and
have restaurants specializing in
making them.

**butter for frying
½ pint (250ml) pancake batter
(see Basic recipes, page 100)
golden or maple syrup**

1. Heat a knob of butter in a
frying pan and pour in sufficient
batter to cover the bottom of the
pan thinly, allow to brown on the
underside, turn and brown on the
other side.
2. Continue in this way until all
the batter is used. As the
pancakes are made, keep them
warm on a plate placed over a
pan of simmering water.
3. Fold each pancake in half and
serve with golden or maple syrup.

DUTCH PANCAKES WITH JAM AND CREAM
Makes 6

**butter for frying
½ pint (250ml) pancake batter
(see Basic recipes, page 100)
strawberry jam
½ pint (250ml) whipped cream
glacé cherries
grated chocolate**

1. Heat knob of butter in a frying
pan, pour in sufficient batter to
cover the bottom of the pan
thinly; allow to brown on the
underside, turn and brown on the
other side.
2. Spread jam and whipped cream
between each pancake, piling one
on top of the other.
3. Decorate the top with whipped
cream, glacé cherries and grated
chocolate.
4. Serve at once, cut into
wedge-shaped portions.

APPLE AND SOURED CREAM BLINTZES
Makes 8

Russia's delicious pancake variation.

6oz (150gm) plain flour
1 teaspoon salt
1 egg
¼ pint (125ml) water
1 carton (5oz or 125gm) soured cream
oil for frying
6 crisp eating apples
1½oz (37gm) butter
1 tablespoon water
½oz (12gm) brown sugar
caster sugar to sprinkle

1. To make batter, sift flour and salt into a bowl, make well in centre and break egg into it. Work flour into egg, adding the ¼ pint (125ml) water at the same time. Beat thoroughly, then stir in soured cream.
2. Cook pancakes in a little oil, until top sets, then turn over to cook the top. Keep pancakes warm.
3. Peel, core and chop apples into ½-inch pieces.
4. Melt ½oz (12gm) of the butter in saucepan, add water and sugar and heat until sugar dissolves.
5. Add apples and cook gently covered with lid, until apples are cooked but still firm. Drain off any liquid.
6. Divide apple mixture equally between pancakes, keeping it in the centre. Fold two opposite sides of pancake into centre and repeat with two remaining sides to form a parcel.
7. To crisp blintzes heat remaining butter in frying pan, taking care not to burn it.
8. Put in four blintzes, folded sides under, and fry until crisp. Turn over and cook other side until crisp. Remove and drain on kitchen paper. Keep warm.
9. Repeat with remaining blintzes.
10. Serve on an oval dish and sprinkle with caster sugar.

PANCAKES NORMANDE
Makes 8

4oz (100gm) flour
2 eggs
pinch of salt
½ pint (250ml) milk
lard or oil for frying
½ pint (250ml) apple purée
2 teaspoons grated lemon rind
juice of ½ lemon
1oz (25gm) large seedless raisins
sugar to taste
lemon slices to decorate

1. Make batter with flour, eggs, salt and milk and allow to stand for 1 hour.
2. Cook spoonfuls of the batter in a frying pan in heated lard or oil, to give thin pancakes. Keep warm.
3. Heat apple purée with lemon rind, juice and raisins. Add sugar to taste.
4. Place a little of the filling on each pancake and roll up.
5. Decorate with lemon slices.

FRENCH APRICOT CREPES
Makes 10

½ pint (250ml) pancake batter (see Basic recipes, page 100)
oil for frying
1 can (2½lb or 1¼ kilo) apricot halves, drained
½ pint (250ml) apricot juice
3 teaspoons arrowroot

1. Make pancakes in the usual way in an omelette pan and stack them up in a clean teatowel.
2. Blend the apricot halves in a liquidizer to a purée, reserving a few halves for decoration. (Or press through a sieve.) Pile a little of this mixture on half of each crepe.
3. Fold the other half over and arrange on a serving dish. Keep warm.
4. Blend a little apricot juice with the arrowroot.
5. Bring the remainder of the juice to the boil.
6. Pour on to the arrowroot and return all the mixture to the pan. Bring to the boil, stirring. Cook for 1-2 minutes.
7. Pour the sauce over the crêpes. Decorate with the reserved apricot halves and serve.

EMPEROR'S OMELETTE
Serves 4

4oz (100gm) flour
pinch of salt
4 egg yolks
½ pint (250ml) milk
4 egg whites
2oz (50gm) butter
few sultanas
sugar to sprinkle

1. Preheat oven to moderate, 350 deg F or gas 4 (180 deg C).
2. Mix flour, salt, egg yolks and milk; stir well to make a smooth batter. Fold in the beaten egg whites.
3. Heat butter in a large fireproof pan, pour in batter, add sultanas, and cook until the underside is set.
4. Place in the centre of the oven and cook until the mixture is set.
5. Divide into four and serve sprinkled with sugar. If liked, serve with stewed plums.

AUSTRIAN RICE SOUFFLE
Serves 4–6

7oz (175gm) round-grain rice
pinch of salt
milk
4½oz (112gm) butter
2¾oz (68gm) sugar
grated rind of 1 lemon
2 egg yolks
2 egg whites
2oz (50gm) raisins
butter
breadcrumbs

1. Preheat oven to moderate, 350 deg F or gas 4 (180 deg C).
2. Boil the rice in salted milk to cover until cooked. If all the milk has not been absorbed, drain.
3. Meanwhile cream the butter and sugar, add the grated lemon rind and the egg yolks and mix well.
4. Mix the rice and raisins together and carefully fold in the stiffly beaten egg whites. Butter an ovenproof mould and sprinkle it with breadcrumbs, pour in the rice mixture and bake in the centre of the oven for 20–30 minutes.
5. Turn out and serve hot with stewed fruit or raspberry juice.

RICE PUDDING PORTUGUESE STYLE
Serves 4

8oz (200gm) round-grain rice
1 pint (approximately ½ litre) milk
lemon peel or vanilla pod
3 egg yolks
cinnamon to decorate

1. Simmer rice and milk together, with the lemon peel or vanilla pod.
2. When the rice is cooked, remove the peel or pod, cool slightly and gradually stir in the egg yolks. Return to the heat and cook, stirring until thickened. (Do not allow to boil after the yolks have been added.)
3. Spoon the mixture into a large flat dish and leave to cool.
4. Sprinkle the top with cinnamon in a criss-cross pattern.

RICE DANISH STYLE
Serves 4

1 pint (approximately ½ litre) milk
4 tablespoons round-grain rice
¼ vanilla pod
8–10 almonds
approximately 1 tablespoon sugar
¼ pint (125ml) double cream
1 tablespoon sherry

1. Rinse a thick-bottomed saucepan and bring the milk to the boil.
2. Wash the rice and place it in the boiling milk, together with the vanilla pod.
3. Stir constantly for the first 5 minutes.
4. Cover the saucepan and turn down the heat, or place an asbestos mat under the pan.
5. Simmer for 45 minutes, stirring occasionally. When cooked remove the vanilla and allow the rice to cool.
6. Meanwhile blanch and chop the almonds.
7. Stir them into the rice together with the sugar.
8. Whip the cream and when the rice is cold, fold in the cream and sherry.
9. Serve in glass dishes with a fruit purée.

AUSTRIAN CHEESE TORTE
Serves 4–6

1lb (½ kilo) cottage cheese
¼ pint (125ml) milk
2oz (50gm) cornflour
3 egg whites
5oz (125gm) sugar
1 teaspoon vanilla essence
2oz (50gm) digestive biscuit crumbs
toasted almonds or double cream and fresh fruit to decorate

1. Preheat oven to moderate, 350 deg F or gas 4 (180 deg C).
2. Sieve the cheese.
3. Blend into it the milk and cornflour.
4. Fold in the beaten egg whites, the sugar and vanilla essence.
5. Brush a loose-bottomed 9-inch (23-cm) cake tin with butter. Sprinkle biscuit crumbs in the base.
6. Spoon in the cheese mixture.
7. Bake in the centre of the oven for 45 minutes.
8. Serve warm, decorated with the toasted almonds, or allow to cool and serve topped with cream and fresh fruit.

ALMOND AND CHERRY CHEESECAKE
Serves 4–6

2 cartons (8oz or 200gm) cottage cheese
1 carton (5oz or 125gm) double cream
3 eggs, separated
2oz (50gm) cornflour
5oz (125gm) caster sugar
few drops of almond essence
2oz (50gm) digestive biscuit crumbs
1 can cherry pie filling

1. Preheat oven to moderate, 350 deg F or gas 4 (180 deg C).
2. Sieve cottage cheese. Blend into it the cream, egg yolks and cornflour.
3. Fold in the whisked egg whites, sugar and almond essence.
4. Brush a loose-bottomed 9-inch (23-cm) cake tin with butter. Sprinkle crumbs in the base. Spoon in the cheese mixture.
5. Bake in the centre of the oven for 45 minutes.
6. Cool slightly and serve topped with the cherry pie filling.

OLD DANISH RUM PUDDING
(Illustrated on page 71)
Serves 4

2 egg yolks
2½oz (62gm) granulated sugar
1oz (25gm) vanilla sugar
1 small glass rum
½ pint (250ml) milk
5 leaves gelatine (or 3 level teaspoons powdered gelatine dissolved in 1 tablespoon hot water)
1 can (6oz or 150gm) cream
1 can (8oz or 200gm) Morello cherries
4 tablespoons water
1 level tablespoon cornflour

1. Whisk the egg yolks, sugar, vanilla sugar and rum in a bowl until thick and frothy.
2. Meanwhile, heat the milk and when it boils, gradually pour it into the egg mixture.
3. Stir in the dissolved gelatine.
4. Leave in a cool place until the rum custard is cold.
5. Whip pre-chilled cream and fold into the rum custard. Pour into a rinsed mould and leave to set.
6. Empty contents of can of cherries into a pan; add half the water and bring to the boil.
8. Dissolve cornflour in remaining water and add to the cherries, stirring.
9. Boil for 2–3 minutes over gentle heat, then leave to cool slightly, and pour over the unmoulded pudding.

SPANISH PUDDING
Serves 4–6

Potatoes and carrots go into this Spanish dessert – a filling dish rather like our Christmas pudding.

8oz (200gm) potato, grated
8oz (200gm) carrot, grated
8oz (200gm) caster sugar
8oz (200gm) raisins or sultanas
8oz (200gm) currants
4oz (100gm) shredded suet
2oz (50gm) self-raising flour
3 eggs
½ teaspoon ground nutmeg

1. Mix all ingredients together.
2. Place in a lightly greased basin, cover and steam for 2½–3 hours.
3. Turn out and serve hot.

SWISS SWEET ROLLS
Serves 4

A dessert dish – *schenkeli* – from Switzerland.

1½oz (37gm) butter
2 eggs
5oz (125gm) sugar
grated rind of 1 lemon
9oz (225gm) flour
fat or oil for deep frying

1. Heat butter in a pan until bubbles appear.
2. Add eggs, sugar and grated lemon rind.
3. Heat the mixture gently, stirring frequently, for about 10 minutes.
4. Gradually mix in flour.
5. Form into finger-sized rolls.
6. Deep fry in heated fat or oil.
7. Drain on absorbent paper and serve with whipped cream.

SWISS PIE WITH CARROTS
Serves 4–6

This idea, using carrots in a dessert pie, comes from Aargau in Switzerland.

5 eggs, separated
8oz (200gm) caster sugar
grated rind and juice of half a lemon
8oz (200gm) almonds, blanched and chopped
8oz (200gm) carrots, grated
pinch of powdered cloves or grated nutmeg
1 teaspoon powdered cinnamon
1½oz (37gm) flour
icing sugar to sprinkle

1. Preheat oven to very moderate, 325 deg F or gas 3 (170 deg C).
2. Whisk the egg yolks with the sugar and lemon rind and juice until thick and creamy.
3. Mix in the almonds, carrots, spices and flour.
4. Fold in the beaten egg whites and spoon into a buttered pie dish.
5. Bake in the centre of the oven for about 1 hour.
6. Allow to cool and serve sprinkled with icing sugar.

SWISS RHUBARB MOUSSE
Serves 4

1lb (½ kilo) rhubarb
5oz (125gm) sugar
3 eggs

1. Dice rhubarb and cook for a few minutes in very little water. Cool slightly then drain in a fine strainer.
2. When cool, put into a saucepan and add the sugar and eggs.
3. Beat well over the heat until smooth, but remove mixture from heat before it boils.
4. Spoon into a serving dish and leave to cool.

HAGUE'S BLUFF
(Illustrated on page 71)
Serves 4–6

A Dutch dessert, *Haagse bluf*, so-called because the Dutch say the people of the Hague are frothy and make much of something small as this dish does.

12 tablespoons raspberry syrup
8oz (200gm) sugar or to taste
4 egg whites

1. Put syrup, sugar and unbeaten egg whites in a large bowl.
2. Whisk for 10 minutes or more (if by hand) to increase the amount.
3. Serve in individual dishes with wafers or sponge finger biscuits.

LOUKOUMADES
Serves 4–6

A traditional Greek dessert.

¾oz (18gm) fresh yeast
1lb (½ kilo) flour
1 teaspoon salt
lukewarm milk or water (see method)
corn oil for deep frying
sugar and cinnamon to sprinkle
honey

1. Dissolve yeast in basin with a little lukewarm milk or water. Add a little of the flour to make a dough.
2. Allow to rise in a warm place, add remaining flour, the salt and enough lukewarm liquid to make a batter soft enough to drop from a spoon.
3. Cover basin and allow to stand for 5–6 hours until it starts to bubble on top.
4. Heat the corn oil and when hot, drop batter from a spoon and fry to a golden colour (dip spoon in a cup of cold water each time to prevent batter sticking to spoon).
5. When loukoumades are risen and golden brown, drain on absorbent paper.
6. Arrange on a dish and sprinkle with sugar and cinnamon. Spoon over a little honey and serve hot.

CHOCOLATE RUM PROFITEROLES WITH ORANGE CREAM FILLING
Makes 30

2oz (50gm) flour
pinch of salt
1½oz (37gm) margarine or butter
scant ¼ pint (125ml) water
2 eggs
3oz (75gm) plain chocolate
2oz (50gm) sugar
1 level teaspoon cocoa powder
¼ pint (125ml) water
1 egg yolk
1–1½ teaspoons rum
½ pint (250ml) double cream
1oz (25gm) icing sugar, sieved
grated rind and juice of 1 orange

1. Preheat oven to moderate to moderately hot, 400 deg F or gas 6 (200 deg C).
2. Sieve together flour and salt.
3. Melt margarine or butter in scant ¼ pint (125ml) water in a large pan and bring to the boil.
4. Remove from heat and beat in sieved flour.
5. Return to heat and beat until paste forms a ball in the pan.
6. Cool slightly and beat in eggs one by one.
7. Pipe walnut-size balls, using ½-inch plain nozzle, on to greased baking sheets. Bake on the top two shelves of the oven for 20 minutes.
9. Make a small hole in the side of each profiterole and return them to oven for further 5 minutes, to dry out. Cool on a wire tray.
10. To make sauce, place chocolate, sugar, cocoa powder and water in a pan and bring slowly to boil.
11. When sugar has dissolved, boil for 20 minutes.
12. Blend a little sauce with egg yolk and return to pan.
13. Return to heat and cook, stirring, without boiling.
14. Add rum and leave to cool.
15. To make filling, whip cream until stiff, fold in sugar and orange rind and juice.
16. Place in piping bag and use to fill profiteroles.
17. To serve, pile profiteroles in serving dish and pour chocolate sauce on top.

MERINGUE DACQUOISE
Serves 6–8

5 egg whites
10oz (250gm) caster sugar
4oz (100gm) almonds, chopped
large pinch of cream of tartar
½ pint (250ml) double cream, whipped
1lb (½ kilo) raspberry purée
grated chocolate to decorate

1. Preheat oven to very cool, 250 deg F or gas ½ (130 deg C).
2. Whisk the egg whites very stiff.
3. Add half the caster sugar and whisk until as stiff as before.
4. Fold in remaining sugar, the almonds and cream of tartar with a metal spoon.
5. Place the mixture in a piping bag fitted with a plain tube.
6. Pipe mixture in two 8-inch (20-cm) rounds on to baking sheets previously covered with bakewell paper.
7. Bake on two lower shelves of the oven for 2½–3 hours.
8. Peel off paper and cool meringue on a wire tray. (The meringue layers can be stored in an airtight tin until ready to use.)
9. Mix together cream and raspberries.
10. Sandwich the two meringue layers together with the raspberry cream.
12. Serve sprinkled with chocolate. (Strawberries, apricots, peaches or blackcurrants may be used instead of raspberries.)

HONEYED GREEK MERINGUES
Serves 6

6 egg whites
12oz (300gm) caster sugar
½ pint (250ml) double cream
2 tablespoons clear honey
4oz (100gm) hazelnuts or almonds, chopped
2 teaspoons brandy or liqueur (optional)

1. Preheat oven to cool, 275 deg F or gas 1 (140 deg C).
2. Whisk the egg whites until very stiff. Whisk in 6 teaspoons of the sugar, then gently fold in the rest of the sugar.
3. Either pipe or drop teaspoonfuls of the mixture on to lightly oiled baking sheets.
4. Bake on the two lower shelves of the oven for 40–45 minutes. Cool on a wire tray.
5. Whip the cream until stiff and fold in the honey, nuts and brandy or liqueur.
6. Just before serving sandwich the meringues with the cream filling and arrange on a dish.

SICILIAN COFFEE SORBET
Serves 4

2 level tablespoons instant coffee granules
4 tablespoons boiling water
2 level tablespoons sugar
½ pint (250ml) cold water
1 carton (5oz or 125gm) double cream

1. Dissolve the instant coffee granules in boiling water.
2. Add the sugar and stir until dissolved.
3. Add the cold water and transfer to an ice tray or foil dish.
4. Freeze in the ice-making compartment of the refrigerator, taking it out from time to time to stir with a fork.
5. When the whole mixture is a crumbly consistency, serve in glasses topped with lightly whipped cream.

Sweetmeats, snacks and drinks

A selection of recipes to delight everyone not on a diet, such as those gorgeous Continental yeast breads, which, although they may take a little time to prepare, are certainly worth the extra effort.

Though the custom of tea and cakes is hardly Continental, the habit of serving tortes with coffee, in the morning or afternoon, is strong in Austria and Germany. They are also served in the evening, after dinner, in Scandinavia and Holland, when guests call.

Cakes or biscuits are cooked for festive occasions, particularly for religious festivals. Russia's *kulich* for Easter is a really elaborate cake that Russian women cosset with hot water bottles while its dough is proving. Swedish St. Lucia cakes, Dutch St. Nicholas letters and Austrian Christmas stollen are all part of the Christmas celebrations. France has superb bakers' confections: croissants, brioches and petits fours and Denmark has its sweet Danish pastries.

Probably the most famous snack in Europe is the Danish open sandwich which makes a meal in itself; the Dutch also love a snack lunch of *uitsmijters* which makes a quick lunch for the housewife.

Drinks can be hot, warming punches from the Alps, or summer soothers like Spain's well-known sangria.

ITALIAN FRUIT LOAF
Serves 4–6

4oz (100gm) glacé cherries
4oz (100gm) mixed nuts
4oz (100gm) sultanas
4oz (100gm) caster sugar
12oz (300gm) self-raising flour
4 tablespoons golden syrup
2 eggs
6 tablespoons milk
Topping:
4oz (100gm) nuts
4oz (100gm) granulated sugar
4 tablespoons water

1. Preheat oven to very moderate, 325 deg F or gas 3 (170 deg C).
2. Prepare a 2-lb (1-kilo) loaf tin by greasing and lining with a double thickness of greaseproof paper.
3. Wash the cherries in hot water, then dry well and chop roughly.
4. Chop the nuts, then mix with the sultanas, sugar, cherries and flour. Make a well in the centre.
5. Measure the golden syrup into a basin, add the eggs and milk.
6. Beat well, then add to the flour, fruit and nuts and mix together.
7. Spoon the mixture into the tin and make the top slightly domed.
8. Bake in the centre of the oven for 1 hour. Turn out and cool on a wire tray.
9. Toast the nuts for the topping lightly under the grill.
10. Heat sugar and water until dissolved, then boil for 1 minute.
11. Remove from the heat and add the nuts, stir well until coated.
12. Spread on top of the loaf and leave to set.

AUSTRIAN COFFEE CAKE
Serves 6–7

4oz (100gm) margarine
4oz (100gm) self-raising flour
½ level teaspoon baking powder
4oz (100gm) caster sugar
1–2 tablespoons coffee essence
2 eggs
¼ pint (125ml) water
4oz (100gm) granulated sugar
4 tablespoons very strong black coffee
1–2 tablespoons brandy
½ pint (250ml) double cream, glacé cherries and flaked almonds to decorate

1. Preheat oven to moderate, 350 deg F or gas 4 (180 deg C).
2. Place the first six ingredients in a mixing bowl and beat together until well blended, 1–2 minutes.
3. Place the mixture in a greased floured 8-inch (20-cm) savarin tin. Smooth the top.
4. Bake in the centre of the oven for 30–35 minutes. Cool on a wire tray.
5. To make the syrup, bring the water to the boil and dissolve the sugar. Boil for 2–3 minutes. Allow to cool slightly and add coffee and brandy.
6. Prick the cake well and spoon the syrup over it. Leave to soak, overnight if possible.
7. To decorate, whip the cream fairly stiffly. Place cake on serving dish and cover top and sides with cream.
8. Place cherries and almonds around the edge.

DANISH SAND CAKE
Serves 8–10

8oz (200gm) butter
8oz (200gm) sugar
5 eggs
8oz (200gm) self-raising flour

1. Preheat oven to very moderate, 325 deg F or gas 3 (170 deg C).
2. Cream the butter and sugar until light and fluffy.
3. Beat in the eggs one at a time then fold in the sieved flour.
4. Spoon into a greased 8-inch (20-cm) cake tin.
5. Bake in the centre of the oven for about 1¼ hours. Turn out and cool on a wire tray.

DANISH SAND BISCUITS
Makes 24

13oz (325gm) butter
1lb (½ kilo) flour
4oz (100gm) caster sugar
3 egg yolks
3 tablespoons water
1 egg white

1. Preheat oven to moderate to moderately hot, 375 deg F or gas 5 (190 deg C).
2. Rub the butter into the flour and add the sugar.
3. Beat the egg yolks with the water and add it to the dry ingredients; knead lightly. Allow the dough to rest in a cool place for 1 hour.
4. Cut the dough into four and roll each piece into a sausage about a ¼ inch thick.
5. Cut into pieces 6 inches long.
6. Take both ends and turn into the centre, crossing at the ends and pressing down.
7. Brush lightly with egg white. Place on greased baking sheets and bake, in batches, in the centre of the oven for 15 minutes until light brown.
8. Cool on a wire tray.

YOGURT GINGER CAKE
Serves 8

4oz (100gm) butter
2oz (50gm) soft brown sugar
2oz (50gm) black treacle
6oz (150gm) golden syrup
1 carton (5oz or 125gm) natural yogurt
2 eggs, beaten
8oz (200gm) plain flour
1 level teaspoon mixed spice
3 level teaspoons ground ginger
½ level teaspoon bicarbonate of soda
3oz (75gm) crystallized ginger, chopped
3oz (75gm) almonds, chopped (optional)

1. Preheat oven to cool, 300 deg F or gas 2 (150 deg C).
2. Warm butter, sugar, treacle and syrup gently together, until butter has melted and sugar dissolved. Cool.
3. Stir in yogurt and beaten eggs.
4. Sieve dry ingredients into a mixing bowl, add cooled mixture and ginger.
5. Add chopped almonds, if used. Blend well.
6. Pour into a greased and lined 7-inch (18-cm) square cake tin and bake in centre of the oven for 1½ hours. Cool on a wire tray.
7. Wrap in foil or greaseproof paper and leave for at least 1 day to mature. Serve with pashka.

PASHKA

A traditional Russian Easter dish which can be served with the yogurt ginger cake.

5 tablespoons double cream
2 teaspoons lemon juice
2½oz (62gm) caster sugar
6oz (150gm) cottage cheese, sieved
1oz (25gm) almonds, blanched and chopped
1oz (25gm) mixed peel
1oz (25gm) seedless raisins
grated rind of half a lemon

1. Sour the cream by stirring in lemon juice and leave to thicken.
2. Stir in sugar, cottage cheese and remaining ingredients.
3. Line a small sieve with muslin and fill with the mixture.
4. Leave in a cool place to drain for 24 hours. A weight can be placed on the mixture in the sieve to force out more liquor.
5. When pashka is solid, remove from mould and serve with the yogurt ginger cake.

DUTCH GINGER BUTTERCAKE
Serves 4–6

7oz (175gm) butter
9oz (225gm) plain flour, sieved
pinch of salt
7oz (175gm) caster sugar
3oz (75gm) crystallized ginger, finely chopped
1 egg, beaten

1. Preheat oven to moderate, 350 deg F or gas 4 (180 deg C).
2. Knead all the ingredients together to form a smooth dough, reserving a little of the egg to glaze.
3. Press into a greased 8-inch (20-cm) cake tin, brush with remaining egg and mark lines with a fork.
4. Cook in the centre of the oven for 40–45 minutes.
5. Leave in the tin for 2–3 minutes, then turn out and cool on a wire tray.

DANISH CHRISTMAS CAKE
Serves 10

In Denmark this cake is served throughout December with the Christmas biscuits (see page 93).

1lb (½ kilo) plain flour
½ teaspoon salt
1 teaspoon ground cinnamon
1 tablespoon sugar
8oz (200gm) mixed dried fruit
¼ pint (125ml) milk
1oz (25gm) fresh yeast
4oz (100gm) butter
2 eggs
loaf sugar, crushed
few flaked almonds

1. Preheat oven to moderate to moderately hot, 400 deg F or gas 6 (200 deg C).
2. Mix flour, salt, cinnamon and sugar together; stir in the mixed dried fruit.
3. Heat the milk until lukewarm.
4. Dissolve yeast in half the milk.
5. Add 3oz (75gm) of the butter to the remaining milk and heat gently to dissolve.
6. Mix both with the beaten eggs and add to the dry ingredients.
7. Beat with the hand until mixture forms a dough in the bowl.
8. Knead well and place in a greased 8-inch (20-cm) square tin.
9. Cover and leave in a warm place for 30 minutes.
10. Melt the remaining butter, brush over the top.
11. Sprinkle the top with crushed sugar and flaked almonds.
12. Bake in the centre of the oven for about 30 minutes. (If liked, this cake may be served buttered.)

KULICH CAKES
Makes 2 large and 2 smaller cakes

Kulich means bird cake and is Russia's Easter cake made in cylindrical tins – each size for a different member of the family. Russian cooks take time and care to make this cake, putting hot water bottles and blankets around it when it is proving and forbidding anyone to enter the kitchen or make too much noise in case the cake collapses!

Yeast batter:
4oz (100gm) plain flour
½oz (12gm) sugar
1oz (25gm) fresh yeast or 1 level tablespoon dried yeast
¼ pint (125ml) warm milk and water

Other ingredients:
12oz (300gm) plain flour
3½oz (87gm) sugar
1 level teaspoon salt
pinch powdered saffron (optional)
2 eggs, beaten
5 tablespoons vegetable oil
½ teaspoon vanilla essence
2oz (50gm) almonds, chopped
2oz (50gm) currants

Decoration:
3 teaspoons warm water
2oz (50gm) icing sugar
½oz (12gm) almonds, chopped
4 chopped glacé cherries

1. Preheat oven to moderate to moderately hot, 375 deg F or gas 5 (190 deg C).
2. Mix flour, sugar, yeast and warm milk together in a large bowl to make batter.
3. Cover with a large polythene bag and leave in a warm place until frothy, about 20 minutes.
4. To make dough, mix together flour, sugar, salt and saffron (if used) and add with eggs, oil, vanilla essence, almonds and currants to yeast batter. Mix well.
5. Turn dough on to a floured surface and knead for 5–10 minutes until smooth. (The dough is very sticky to begin with but tightens up on kneading.)
6. Place dough in a lightly oiled large polythene bag, loosely tied, and leave until double in size and dough springs back when pressed with a floured finger. It will take about 1½–2 hours in a warm place.
7. Remove from bag and knead for 1–2 minutes.
8. Cut off enough dough to half

fill well greased cans (use empty, well cleaned soup, fruit, cocoa or beer cans in varying sizes – as a guide 6oz (150gm) dough for 12 fl oz can, 4oz (100gm) for 6–8 fl oz can and 3oz (75gm) dough for 5 fl oz can).
9. Cover cans with polythene bag and leave to rise until dough is about 1 inch from the top of the cans.
10. Bake for 30–45 minutes according to size of can. Remove carefully from cans and cool.
11. To decorate, mix water with icing sugar and spoon over top of *kulichs*.
12. Decorate tops with chopped almonds and cherries.

LINZERTORTE
Serves 4–6

This originally came from the Upper Austrian town of Linz, though long associated with Vienna.

6oz (150gm) plain flour
½ level teaspoon cinnamon
3oz (75gm) butter
2oz (50gm) sugar
2oz (50gm) ground almonds
grated rind and juice of 1 lemon
2 egg yolks
12oz (300gm) raspberry jam

1. Preheat oven to moderate to moderately hot, 375 deg F or gas 5 (190 deg C).
2. Sieve flour and cinnamon into a bowl.
3. Rub in butter until mixture resembles fine breadcrumbs.
4. Add sugar, ground almonds and lemon rind.
5. Beat eggs and add to flour mixture with sufficient lemon juice to bind to a stiff dough.
6. Knead lightly and leave in a cool place for 30 minutes.
7. Press two-thirds of the dough into a 7-inch (18-cm) fluted flan ring, placed on a baking sheet.
9. Fill with raspberry jam.
10. Roll out remaining pastry and cut into ½-inch strips.
11. Use to make a lattice design over the jam. Bake for about 25–30 minutes in centre of oven.
12. Leave to cool before removing flan ring. Serve with cream. (Instead of jam, 1lb (½ kilo) fresh or frozen raspberries may be used, cooked with 1 tablespoon water and ½oz (12gm) butter.)

SACHERTORTE
Serves 4–6

The famous Viennese chocolate cake created by the Sacher Hotel.

6oz (150gm) butter
6oz (150gm) sugar
6½oz (162gm) semi-sweet
chocolate, melted
8 egg yolks
8oz (200gm) plain flour
8 egg whites

Chocolate icing:
8oz (200gm) sugar
scant ¼ pint (125ml) water
7oz (175gm) semi-sweet
chocolate
apricot jam

1. Preheat oven to cool, 275 deg F or gas 1 (140 deg C).
2. Beat butter until creamy, add the sugar and melted chocolate. Beat in the egg yolks, one at a time, adding a little of the flour with every egg after the first. Fold in the remaining flour and the stiffly whisked egg whites.
3. Spoon into a greased 9-inch (23-cm) cake tin. Bake in the centre of the oven for 1–1½ hours. (Test with a needle, if it comes out cleanly, the cake is cooked.)
4. Cool on a wire tray.
5. Make the icing, cook the sugar and water to a thin thread consistency. Melt the chocolate in a bowl, placed over a pan of hot water.
6. Add the sugar gradually to the melted chocolate, stirring all the time. Continue stirring until the icing coats the back of the spoon.
7. Slice the cake in half, through the centre, and sandwich together with apricot jam.
8. Pour the chocolate icing on top of the cake, quickly smooth it over the top and around the sides.
9. Serve with whipped cream.

ITALIAN TORRONE
(Illustrated on page 71)
Makes 12–16 slices

4oz (100gm) soft margarine
3oz (75gm) cocoa powder
5oz (125gm) ground almonds
1 egg
4oz (100gm) caster sugar
2 tablespoons water
2oz (50gm) semi-sweet biscuits
1oz (25gm) glacé cherries,
chopped
1oz (25gm) walnuts, chopped
walnut halves and 2 glacé
cherries to decorate

1. Mix margarine and cocoa powder together until soft.
2. Add ground almonds and egg, mix in well.
3. Place sugar and water in a saucepan and dissolve gently.
4. Pour on to cocoa mixture and beat well.
5. Break biscuits into almond-size pieces and add to the mixture, together with cherries and walnuts.
6. Place in an 8-inch (20-cm) sandwich tin lined with greaseproof paper; smooth top with a knife and leave to set in a refrigerator or cold place.
7. Ease around the edge with a knife and turn out on to a plate.
8. Decorate with walnuts and glacé cherries and serve immediately, or return to refrigerator until required.

FLORENTINES
Makes about 20

2oz (50gm) butter
4oz (100gm) sugar
1 tablespoon honey
1 teaspoon lemon juice
2oz (50gm) plain flour
4oz (100gm) mixed chopped peel
2oz (50gm) almonds, chopped
3oz (75gm) each of milk and
bitter chocolate

1. Preheat oven to moderate, 350 deg F or gas 4 (180 deg C).
2. Put butter, sugar, honey and lemon juice in a small pan and place over a low heat, to melt the butter. Remove from heat.
3. Mix the flour, peel and almonds together and add to the melted ingredients.
4. Grease baking sheets and drop teaspoonfuls of the mixture on to them, leaving room for the biscuits to spread.
5. Pat each biscuit down very firmly with a spatula.
6. Bake on the two lower shelves of the oven for 10 minutes, until edges are crispy.
7. Cool on a wire tray. Melt the two types of chocolate together over hot water and spread over the bottom of the biscuits.
8. Store in an airtight tin with foil between the layers.

PETITS-FOURS

The following four recipes are for small French-style bisuits, usually served in sweet paper cases, eaten after dinner with the coffee.

JAP FINGERS
Makes about 8

1 egg white
2oz (50gm) caster sugar
1½oz (37gm) ground almonds

1. Preheat oven to cool, 275 deg F or gas 1 (140 deg C).
2. Whisk egg white, add sugar and fold in ground almonds.
3. Using a ½-inch plain tube, pipe fingers and rounds on to bakewell or waxed paper placed on a baking sheet.
4. Bake in the centre of the oven for 45 minutes–1 hour.

CECILIAS
Makes about 8

2oz (50gm) caster sugar
2oz (50gm) ground almonds
1 teaspoon sherry
egg white to bind
melted chocolate and green
glacé icing to decorate

1. Mix together sugar, almonds and sherry and add sufficient egg white to bind.
2. Using a ½-inch plain tube, pipe rounds and fingers on to bakewell or waxed paper.
3. Leave to set.
4. Cover some with glacé icing and dip rest in melted chocolate

MACAROONS
Makes about 8

2oz (50gm) caster sugar
2oz (50gm) ground almonds
few drops almond essence
1 egg white
flaked almonds

1. Preheat oven to very moderate, 325 deg F or gas 3 (170 deg C).
2. Mix sugar, almonds, essence together and bind to a soft piping consistency with egg white.
3. Using a ½-inch plain tube, pipe into rounds, on bakewell or waxed paper, placed on a baking sheet.
4. Press a flaked almond on top of each.
5. Bake in the centre of the oven for 10–15 minutes.

TRUFFLES
Makes 8–12

2oz (50gm) margarine, melted
2oz (50gm) ground almonds
2oz (50gm) caster sugar
2oz (50gm) plain chocolate, melted
rum to taste
chocolate vermicelli

1. Mix margarine, almonds, sugar, chocolate and rum together.
2. Allow mixture to set.
3. Roll into balls and coat with chocolate vermicelli.

LUCIA BUNS
Makes 24

It is the custom on December 13 (St. Lucia's day) in Sweden for the eldest daughter, wearing a candle and greenery crown, to bring coffee and these buns to her parents for breakfast.

¼ pint (125ml) milk
pinch saffron
2oz (50gm) margarine or butter
3oz (75gm) sugar
1lb 2oz (450gm) plain flour
1 level teaspoon salt
Yeast liquid:
blend 1oz (25gm) fresh yeast in ¼ pint (125ml) water or dissolve 1 teaspoon sugar in ¼ pint (125ml) warm water and sprinkle 1 level tablespoon dried yeast on top. Leave until frothy, about 10 minutes.

1 egg
2oz (50gm) raisins
1 egg beaten with water and a little sugar to glaze
few raisins to decorate

1. Preheat oven to moderate to moderately hot, 400 deg F or gas 6 (200 deg C).
2. Heat milk and mix in saffron.
3. Add butter or margarine and sugar and stir until fat has melted. Cool.
4. In a second bowl, mix 1lb (½ kilo) flour with salt.
5. Add milk mixture, yeast liquid, egg and raisins and beat well together to make a soft dough.
6. Turn out on to the remaining flour on a board and knead it with the hands until you get a smooth elastic ball.
7. Put to rise in a lightly oiled polythene bag or an 8-inch (20-cm) saucepan with lid, at room temperature for about 2 hours. (A slow rise gives a better result with this dough.)
8. Turn the dough on to a lightly floured board.
9. Knead and divide into three pieces, keeping the dough you are not working with covered.
10. To shape pieces as **Lucia cats**, divide dough into 12 pieces and roll each piece into a 9-inch long strip. Lightly flour a baking sheet lay two strips side by side, pinch centres together and coil outwards.
11. For **Lucia buns**, divide as above, roll to 9-inch strips. Place on a baking sheet, cross the strips

to make an X. Curl each end into a small coil in the same direction.
12. For **Twists**, divide dough as above. Roll into 9-inch strips. Place on a baking sheet and shape into an S, coiling each end.
13. Press a raisin in centre of each coil.
14. Put baking sheets in a lightly oiled polythene bags.
15. Leave to rise in a warm place until buns are light and puffy, about 20 minutes.
16. Glaze with egg mixture and bake towards top of the oven for 10–15 minutes until golden brown.
17. Cool on a wire tray.

SWEDISH CHRISTMAS SPICY SNAPS
Makes about 60

5oz (125gm) butter or margarine
6oz (150gm) light brown sugar
2 tablespooons black treacle
3 tablespoons boiled water, cooled
1 teaspoon grated lemon rind
1¼lb (600gm) flour, sieved
1 teaspoon bicarbonate of soda
1 tablespoon cinnamon
1½ teaspoons ground cloves
1 teaspoon ground cardamon seeds
glacé icing (optional)

1. Preheat oven to moderate, 350 deg F or gas 4 (180 deg C).
2. Cream butter or margarine and sugar thoroughly.
3. Add black treacle, water and lemon rind.
4. Sieve flour with bicarbonate of soda and spices. Add to creamed mixture a little at a time. Blend well.
5. Flour hands, toss dough quickly on floured surface and place in refrigerator; chill.
6. Turn dough on to floured surface. Roll out very thinly and cut into shapes with floured biscuit cutters.
7. Bake on buttered baking sheets and bake on the top two shelves of the oven for 8–10 minutes. Cool biscuits on sheet.
8. If liked, the tops of these biscuits can be spread with a little glacé icing.

BUCHE DE NOEL

A French Christmas cake.

2½lb (1¼ kilo) chestnuts
1 vanilla pod
8oz (200gm) dessert chocolate
3½oz (87gm) unsalted butter

1. Wash the chestnuts. Make a slit with a knife in their shells.
2. Place them in a pan of boiling water. Blanch for 10 minutes.
3. Remove the outer shell and the inner brown skin.
4. Return them to the pan with clean boiling water to which the vanilla pod has been added. Cook until tender.
5. Remove the vanilla pod.
6. Drain and sieve, or pass chestnuts through a vegetable mill.
7. Meanwhile, melt the chocolate in a bowl placed over a pan of hot water.
8. Beat the softened butter into the chestnut purée and while it is still warm stir in the melted chocolate.
9. Leave in a cool place to harden slightly, then form into a log shape.
10. Cut off each end diagonally.
11. Mark with a fork to resemble the bark of a tree and decorate with a cluster of artificial holly berries and small meringue 'mushrooms'. (This cake should be eaten within 2-3 days' of making, as this chestnut mixture does not keep well.)

GARLAND STOLLEN

Austria's and Germany's decorative cake for Christmas.

Batter ingredients:
2oz (50gm) plain flour
½ teaspoon sugar
¼oz (6gm) fresh yeast or 1 level teaspoon dried yeast
¼ pint (125ml) warm milk

Additional ingredients:
3oz (75gm) butter
2oz (50gm) caster sugar
1 egg
6oz (150gm) plain flour
½ teaspoon salt
3oz (75gm) raisins
1oz (25gm) almonds, chopped
grated rind of half a lemon
1oz (25gm) mixed peel

Filling:
½oz (12gm) butter, melted
3oz (75gm) glacé cherries, chopped or 3 tablespoons mincemeat

Decoration:
glacé icing
crystallized orange slices

1. Preheat oven to moderate, 350 deg F or gas 4 (180 deg C).
2. Mix the 2oz (50gm) flour, ½ teaspoon sugar, yeast and warm milk to batter in a large bowl.
3. Cover and leave batter for 20-30 minutes, in a warm place, to become frothy.
4. Cream butter and sugar, add the egg and beat well.
5. Add creamed mixture to the frothy batter with the rest of the flour, the salt, fruit, nuts, lemon rind and mixed peel.
6. Mix to make a dough. Cover the bowl with a lightly greased polythene bag. Leave to rise until double its size, 1½-2 hours, in a warm place – or for longer if in a cool one.
7. Turn the dough on to a lightly floured board and knead well.
8. Shape into an oval about 12 inches by 8 inches and brush with melted butter.
9. Spread on the filling and fold over lengthwise so that the top layer is 1 inch from the edge of the bottom.
10. Put the stollen on a floured baking sheet and cover with greased polythene.
11. Allow to rise until dough springs back when pressed with a lightly floured finger – 45 minutes in a warm place.
12. Remove the polythene.
13. Brush stollen with melted butter and bake in the centre of the oven for 45-55 minutes.
14. Cool on a wire tray, then decorate the top with glacé icing and crystallized orange slices.

GUGELHUPF
Serves 8

A well-known German yeast cake.

12oz (300gm) plain flour
2oz (50gm) almonds, chopped
1oz (25gm) fresh yeast
1oz (25gm) caster sugar
½ pint (250ml) lukewarm milk
½ teaspoon salt
3 eggs
4oz (100gm) butter, melted
4oz (100gm) currants and raisins
icing sugar to sprinkle

1. Preheat oven to moderate to moderately hot, 400 deg F or gas 6 (200 deg C).
2. Grease ring mould and sprinkle with a little flour, then sprinkle with the almonds.
3. Cream the yeast with sugar and a little of the warm milk.
4. Put the remaining flour and the salt in a mixing bowl, make a well in the centre and add the beaten eggs, melted butter and yeast mixture.
5. Stir well together, then finally add the fruit and mix with the remainder of the milk.
6. Pour the mixture into the prepared tin which should not be more than three-quarters full.
7. Cover and put the mould into a warm place until the dough rises to the top of the tin.
8. Bake in the centre of the oven for 45 minutes–1 hour.
9. Turn out on to a wire tray, cool and sprinkle with icing sugar.

DUTCH DOUGHNUTS
Makes 20

These doughnuts – *oliebollen* – are eaten on New Year's Eve in Holland served with coffee or liqueurs.

¾oz (18gm) fresh yeast
½ pint (250ml) milk
1¼lb (600gm) plain flour
1 teaspoon salt
1 egg
1lb 1½oz (437gm) currants and raisins mixed
1 tart apple
oil for deep frying

1. Blend yeast with a little lukewarm milk.
2. Sieve flour and salt, add milk, yeast liquid and egg.
3. Add currants, raisins and peeled and minced apple. Beat the mixture well.
4. Cover and leave batter in warm place to rise to double its size.
5. Heat oil.
6. Form batter, with two metal spoons, into balls and carefully drop them into heated oil.
7. Fry for approximately 3–4 minutes, until brown and risen.
8. Drain on absorbent paper. Serve hot, sprinkled with icing sugar.

SPICY BISCUITS
Makes 18

These biscuits – *janhagel* – are popular in Holland.

4oz (100gm) butter
6oz (150gm) plain flour
2oz (50gm) caster sugar
½ teaspoon cinnamon
1oz (25gm) almonds, chopped
1oz (25gm) granulated sugar

1. Preheat oven to moderate, 350 deg F or gas 4 (180 deg C).
2. Rub butter into sieved flour, caster sugar and cinnamon and knead mixture together.
3. Press into a buttered Swiss roll tin, flatten with a knife.
4. Sprinkle with chopped almonds and granulated sugar.
5. Bake in the centre of the oven for 20–25 minutes, until golden brown.
6. Cut into 18 fingers while still warm and finish cooling on a wire tray.

BOTERLETTER
(Illustrated on page 71)
Serves 4–6

Pastry:
8oz (200gm) plain flour
6oz (150gm) butter
scant ¼ pint (125ml) water

Almond paste:
6oz (150gm) ground almonds
6oz (150gm) caster sugar
1 egg
juice of half a lemon
almond essence
beaten egg to glaze
½oz (12gm) angelica, 2 glacé cherries to decorate

1. Preheat oven to hot, 425 deg F or gas 7 (220 deg C).
2. Make pastry with flour, butter and water. Roll into a long strip approximately 4 inches wide and ⅛ inch thick.
3. Mix almond paste ingredients together and form into a long sausage shape, using your hands, and making it just a little shorter than the length of pastry. Place on top of the pastry strip. Wrap pastry around the paste, sealing the edge and ends with beaten egg. Place on a baking sheet and form into the shape of a letter.
4. Glaze with beaten egg. Bake in the centre of the oven for approximately 30 minutes.
5. When golden brown, remove from the oven and allow to cool. Decorate with chopped angelica and glacé cherries and serve, cut in slices, with tea or coffee.

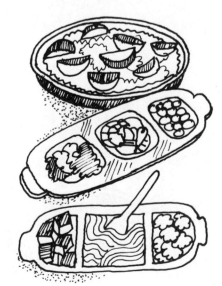

DANISH CHRISTMAS BISCUITS

8oz (200gm) plain flour
½ teaspoon baking powder
5oz (125gm) butter
3oz (75gm) caster sugar
2 tablespoons beaten egg

1. Preheat oven to moderate to moderately hot, 375 deg F or gas 5 (190 deg C).
2. Sieve flour and baking powder.
3. Rub in butter until mixture resembles breadcrumbs.
4. Stir in the sugar and add egg to make a soft dough.
5. Divide into three equal portions and shape as follows.

Finnish bread (*Finskbrod*)
Makes 18

Roll out one portion of the dough into a long sausage about 1½ inches wide. Pass the rolling pin over the top to flatten slightly. Cut into ½-inch slices, slantwise. Place on greased baking sheets and bake in the centre of the oven until firm and pale honey in colour, about 15 minutes.

Jewish cakes (*Jodekager*)
Makes 26

Roll out another portion very thinly on a sheet of greaseproof. Cut into rounds with a 1½-inch plain cutter. Brush with beaten egg and sprinkle with a mixture of cinnamon, sugar and chopped blanched almonds. Bake on the second shelf of the oven until firm, 10–12 minutes.

Vanilla rings (*Vaniljekranse*)
Makes 25

Into the remaining dough beat 1oz (25gm) butter, 1oz (25gm) finely chopped or ground almonds, and ½ teaspoon vanilla essence. Place in a forcing bag with medium star tube. Pipe into rings, about 2 inches in diameter, on a lightly greased baking sheet. Bake on the second shelf of the oven until firm and honey in colour, about 10 minutes.

BOTER MOPPEN
Makes about 30

Boter moppen and *sprits* are typical Dutch biscuits, nationally popular.

6oz (150gm) butter
5oz (125gm) granulated sugar
few drops vanilla essence
8oz (200gm) plain flour

1. Preheat oven to moderate to moderately hot, 375 deg F or gas 5 (190 deg C).
2. Cream the butter and sugar and add the vanilla essence.
3. Stir in the flour.
4. Sprinkle a board with the sugar and roll the mixture into a sausage shape.
5. Cool, in the refrigerator, until the mixture is really firm.
6. Cut into slices, place on a baking sheet and bake in the centre of the oven for approximately 20–30 minutes, until pale brown at the edges.

SPRITS
Makes about 25

6oz (150gm) butter
4oz (100gm) caster sugar
few drops vanilla essence
4 teaspoons beaten egg
8oz (200gm) plain flour

1. Preheat oven to moderate, 350 deg F or gas 4 (180 deg C).
2. Cream the butter and sugar until light and fluffy.
3. Add the vanilla essence and egg.
4. Stir in the flour.
5. Using a large rose nozzle, pipe the mixture on to greased baking sheets to form long narrow strips, 1½ inches wide.
6. The lines of piping should go across the width of the strip.
7. Cool the mixture in the refrigerator before baking.
8. Bake in the centre of the oven for 15–20 minutes, until pale golden brown.
9. Cut into fingers while still warm.

DUTCH EASTER MEN
Makes 6

2lb (1 kilo) plain flour
1oz (25gm) butter
1oz (25gm) fresh yeast
1 teaspoon sugar
1 pint (approximately ½ litre) tepid milk
6 eggs
12 currants
glacé cherries and angelica
beaten egg to glaze

1. Preheat oven to hot, 450 deg F or gas 8 (230 deg C).
2. Sieve the warmed flour and rub in the butter.
3. Cream the yeast with the sugar and add the milk.
4. Make a well in the flour and pour in the liquid.
5. Beat with the hand until the dough leaves the sides of the bowl and the hand is left clean. Knead well.
6. Cover the bowl and leave in a warm place until the dough is doubled in size, about 1 hour.
7. Turn on to a floured board and knead.
8. Divide the mixture into six pieces and form each into an oblong shape.
9. Place the raw egg, in its shell, in the centre of each piece of dough. Imagine that the egg is the centre of a clock face and, using a knife, cut the dough in slits at 2, 4, 6, 8 and 10 o'clock.
10. Pull the dough to form arms and legs and mould the head.
11. Make the eyes with currants, nose with angelica, and mouth with a piece of glacé cherry.
12. Fold arms over the egg.
13. Place men on a greased baking sheet, cover and prove for 20–30 minutes in a warm place.
14. Glaze with beaten egg and bake in the centre of the oven for approximately 30 minutes. Serve warm with butter.

DUTCH EASTER BREAD
Serves 6

Bread with almond paste is a traditional part of Easter in Holland.

½oz (12gm) fresh yeast
1 teaspoon sugar
½ pint (250ml) milk
12oz (300gm) plain flour
1 level teaspoon mixed spice
6oz (150gm) currants and sultanas
1oz (25gm) chopped candied peel
1oz (25gm) butter, melted

Almond paste:
3oz (75gm) ground almonds
1 egg yolk
3oz (75gm) caster sugar
1 teaspoon lemon juice
milk to glaze

1. Preheat oven to hot, 425 deg F or gas 7 (220 deg C).
2. Cream yeast and sugar together and add the warmed milk.
3. Mix into warmed sieved flour and spice from a well in the centre.
4. Knead together and cover bowl with a damp cloth; put to rise in a warm place for approximately 30 minutes.
5. Knock back the dough, work in dried fruit and melted butter.
6. Make the almond paste by mixing the ground almonds, egg yolk, sugar and lemon juice together.
7. Shape dough into an oblong 10 inches by 5 inches and place a sausage shape of almond paste 9½ inches long on top of the dough.
8. Press the dough around the almond paste, tucking the join underneath.
9. Place on a baking sheet and prove, in a warm place, until double in bulk.
10. Glaze with milk and bake in the centre of the oven for 10 minutes, and then for a further 45 minutes in a moderate oven, 350 deg F or gas 4 (180 deg C) until evenly browned and a hollow sound is obtained when the loaf is tapped on the underside. Allow to cool on a wire tray.
11. Slice and spread with butter.

BRIOCHE
Makes 12

Yeast liquid:
½oz (12gm) fresh yeast blended into ¼ tablespoon cold water or 2 level teaspoons dried yeast and ½ level teaspoon caster sugar sprinkled on 1½ tablespoons warm water.
Leave until frothy – about 10 minutes

Other ingredients:
8oz (200gm) plain flour
½ level teaspoon salt
½oz (12gm) caster sugar
2 eggs, beaten
2oz (50gm) butter, melted and cooled

Glaze:
1 egg, beaten
1 tablespoon water
pinch of salt

1. Preheat oven to hot, 450 deg F or gas 8 (230 deg C).
2. Prepare yeast liquid as above.
3. Sieve together flour, salt and sugar into a large bowl.
4. Add yeast liquid, eggs and butter and work to a soft dough.
5. Turn on to a lightly floured surface and knead well for about 5 minutes.
6. Place dough in a lightly greased large polythene bag and allow to rise at room temperature for 1–1½ hours.
7. Grease 12 3-inch brioche tins or deep bun tins with melted lard.
8. Divide risen dough into four equal pieces and then each of them into three pieces.
9. Shape about three-quarters of each piece into a ball and put in the tin.
10. Firmly press a hole in the centre and place remaining piece of dough, shaped as a ball, in the centre.
11. Repeat with remaining pieces and place all the tins on a baking sheet.
12. Put inside a large greased polythene bag and leave to rise until double in size, about 1 hour in a warm place.
13. Blend together all ingredients for glaze.
14. Brush over the brioches and bake in centre of the oven for 10 minutes. Serve warm.

DANISH PASTRIES
Makes 8–9

1oz (25gm) fresh or 1 level tablespoon dried yeast
2oz (50gm) sugar
½ pint (250ml) tepid milk or water
1lb (½ kilo) plain flour, sifted
6oz (150gm) lard
1 egg, beaten

Fillings:
3oz (75gm) cherries, chopped and 3oz (75gm) raisins; 2 tablespoons almonds, chopped and 2 tablespoons honey; 3oz (75gm) ground almonds and 1 egg white; juice of ½ lemon and 3oz (75gm) cake crumbs; 3 tablespoons chopped apricots and 1 tablespoon brown sugar milk to glaze
lemon curd, glacé icing, chopped nuts, glacé cherries and angelica to decorate

1. Preheat oven to hot, 425 deg F or gas 7 (220 deg C).
2. Cream yeast with 1 teaspoon of sugar, and about three-quarters of the liquid and sprinkle surface lightly with some of the flour. (Follow manufacturer's instructions for dried yeast.)
3. Leave in a warm place for 20 minutes until bubbles appear on the surface.
4. Rub 2oz (50gm) lard into remaining flour and sugar, add yeast mixture and egg and work to a soft elastic dough, adding more liquid if needed.
5. Knead until smooth, cover with a cloth and leave to rise until double in size – about 1 hour.
6. Knead again lightly, roll to an oblong about ½ inch thick.
7. Spread two-thirds of the dough with half remaining lard, fold into three, give a half turn and roll out again. Repeat with rest of lard.
8. Mix chosen filling ingredients together. Roll dough ¼ inch thick and shape pastries as required, folding or rolling around filling. Place on a baking sheet.
9. Leave for 30 minutes, in a warm place, brush lightly with milk and bake in the centre of the oven for 12–15 minutes.
10. While still warm, brush with melted lemon curd or glacé icing and decorate with nuts, glacé cherries and angelica.

CROISSANTS
Makes 12

Dry mix:
1lb ($\frac{1}{2}$ kilo) plain flour
2 level teaspoons salt
1oz (25gm) lard

Yeast liquid:
1oz (25gm) fresh yeast blended into $\frac{1}{2}$ pint (250ml) less 4 tablespoons water or 1 level tablespoon dried yeast and 1 teaspoon sugar sprinkled on $\frac{1}{2}$ pint (250ml) less 4 tablespoons warm water. Leave until frothy, about 10 minutes.
1 egg, beaten
4–6oz (100–150gm) hard margarine

Glaze:
1 egg, beaten
1 tablespoon water
$\frac{1}{2}$ teaspoon sugar

1. Preheat oven to hot, 425 deg F or gas 7 (220 deg C).
2. Make a dough with dry mix, yeast liquid and beaten egg.
3. Knead on a lightly floured board, until dough is smooth, 10–15 minutes.
4. Roll dough into a strip a $\frac{1}{4}$ inch thick and approximately 20 inches by 8 inches, taking care to keep the edges straight and the corners square.
4. Soften margarine with a knife then divide into three. Use one part to dot top two-thirds of dough, leaving a small border clear. Fold in three by bringing up plain bottom third first, then folding top third over. Turn dough so that fold is on right hand side. Seal edges with a rolling pin.
5. Re-shape to a long strip by gently pressing dough at intervals with a rolling pin. Repeat with other two portions of margarine.
6. Place in a greased polythene bag and allow to rest in refrigerator for 30 minutes.
7. Roll out, as before, and repeat folding and rolling three times more. Place in refrigerator for at least 1 hour.
8. Roll dough to a rectangle about 23 inches by 14 inches. Cover with lightly greased polythene and leave for 10 minutes.
9. Trim with a knife to 21 inches by 12 inches and divide into half lengthwise.
10. Cut each strip into six

triangles 6 inches high with a 6-inch base.
11. Brush with glaze, roll up each triangle loosely towards point, finishing with tip underneath. Curve into croissant shape.
12. After shaping, put croissants on an ungreased baking sheet. Brush tops with glaze, put baking sheet inside a lightly greased polythene bag and leave at room temperature for about 30 minutes until light and puffy.
13. Brush again with glaze before baking, in centre of oven, for 20 minutes. Serve warm if possible.

SPANISH CHOCOLATE FRIED BREAD
(Illustrated on page 72)
Serves 4

A great favourite in Spain where it is known as *torrijas*.

stale bread slices, $\frac{1}{2}$ inch thick
1 egg yolk
$\frac{1}{2}$ pint (250ml) milk
1 tablespoon sherry
butter for frying
caster sugar
grated chocolate

1. Cut the bread into fingers about 1 inch wide.
2. Beat the egg yolk and add the milk and sherry.
3. Dip the bread into this, drain and fry until golden in the butter.
4. Drain on absorbent paper, sprinkle with caster sugar and cover with grated chocolate, reserving some to decorate.
5. Pile on to a dish and sprinkle with chocolate.
6. Serve very hot.

CHEESE SUPPER SANDWICHES
Serves 3

These are called *kaasteefjes* and are often served in Holland.

2oz (50gm) softened butter
2 tablespoons made mustard
6 slices white bread, $\frac{1}{2}$ inch thick
Edam or Gouda cheese slices
1 egg
$\frac{1}{4}$ pint (125ml) milk
$\frac{1}{4}$ teaspoon salt
pinch of pepper
butter for frying

1. Blend butter and mustard and spread on trimmed slices of bread.
2. Cover three slices with slices of cheese, top with remaining bread slices.
3. Dip sandwiches in mixture of beaten egg, milk, salt and pepper.
4. Fry in butter until golden on both sides. Drain on absorbent paper and serve hot.

EGGS AND HAM DUTCH STYLE
Serves 3

A typical Dutch lunch or snack dish – *uitsmijters*.

butter
6 slices white bread
6 eggs
12 slices ham or roast beef
salt and pepper
mustard
pickles

1. Butter all slices of bread, put two slices of ham or roast beef on each slice, which should more than cover the bread.
2. Fry the eggs lightly and place one on top of each piece of meat.
3. Serve two on each plate with seasoning, mustard and pickles.

SMORREBROD OR DANISH OPEN SANDWICHES
(Illustrated on page 72)

A national habit delightful for lunch or casual supper. The custom is said to have originated from the days when the poor served food on bread rather than plates. Various ingredients can be used, according to what is available, and the number of servings is also flexible. Here are some suggestions.

BACON AND PATE

1 can (2¼oz or 56gm) pâté de foie truffe
slices wholemeal bread or rye bread, buttered
sliced sweet sour pickled gherkin
peeled and sliced cucumber
sliced radishes
black olives
rolled, grilled streaky bacon
button mushrooms, canned or fresh (if fresh, sauté in butter)
watercress

1. Spread the pâté on to two pieces of bread.
2. Garnish one piece with slices of gherkin, cucumber, radish and black olives.
3. Garnish the second piece with rolls of grilled bacon, button mushrooms and watercress.
4. Repeat until you have the number of sandwiches you require.

HORSERADISH AND LUNCHEON MEAT

1 can (7oz or 175gm) pork luncheon meat, sliced
slices wholemeal or rye bread, buttered
horseradish cream
orange slices
black olives

1. Place a slice of pork luncheon meat on a piece of bread.
2. Garnish with horseradish cream, a slice of orange and black olives.
3. Repeat until you have the number of sandwiches you require.

HAM AND RUSSIAN SALAD

1 can (1lb or ½ kilo) ham, sliced
slices of wholemeal or rye bread, buttered
Russian salad (vegetables in mayonnaise)
tomato quarters
mustard and cress

1. Put a slice of ham on to a piece of bread, garnish with Russian salad, tomato quarters and mustard and cress.
2. Repeat until you have the number of sandwiches you require.

HAM, RUSSIAN SALAD AND RED PEPPER

1 can (7oz or 175gm) chopped ham with pork, sliced
slices wholemeal or rye bread, buttered
Russian salad
red pepper slices

1. Place a slice of chopped ham with pork on to a piece of the buttered bread.
2. Decorate with Russian salad and red pepper.
3. Repeat until you have the number of sandwiches you require.

SCRAMBLED EGG AND SAUSAGE

scrambled egg
slices of wholemeal or rye bread, buttered
1 can (4oz or 100gm) cocktail sausages, drained
red pepper strips

1. Put scrambled egg on a slice of the buttered bread and place cocktail sausages on top, garnish with strips of pepper.
2. Repeat until you have the number of sandwiches you require.

SCRAMBLED EGG AND BACON

3 eggs
2 tablespoons milk
salt and pepper
1oz (25gm) margarine
4 slices pumpernickel bread
butter or margarine for spreading
4 lettuce leaves
8 bacon rashers, crisply fried
1 tomato, sliced

1. To make scrambled eggs, mix eggs, milk, salt and pepper together. Melt margarine in a saucepan, pour in egg mixture and cook gently over a low heat, stirring all the time. When the eggs have thickened and set leave to cool on a plate.
2. Spread pumpernickel bread with butter or margarine. Place a large lettuce leaf on the bread and place egg down the centre.
3. Arrange two rashers of bacon across egg and garnish with slices of tomato.

STUFFED HAM SANDWICH

1 dessert apple
1oz (25gm) walnuts, finely chopped
1 tablespoon mayonnaise
4 slices ham
4 slices rye bread
margarine for spreading
4 lettuce leaves
4 gherkins

1. Peel, core and cut apple into small pieces.
2. Mix with walnuts and mayonnaise.
3. Cut slices of ham in half.
4. Place filling near one end of ham and form into a roll.
5. Cover buttered slices of rye bread with a lettuce leaf.
6. Place two ham rolls on each slice and garnish with gherkin fan. (To make the fan, make three cuts, not quite through to the ends, lengthwise, and spread out like a fan.)

THE BEEFEATER

2 slices underdone roast beef
buttered bread
lettuce
1 dessertspoon horseradish cream
fried onions
fresh horseradish (optional)
gherkin
tomato

1. Arrange the beef on the buttered bread.
2. Place a piece of lettuce at one end.
3. Spoon the horseradish cream in the centre.
4. Add a scattering of fried onions.
5. If liked, sprinkle a little freshly grated horseradish on to the horseradish cream.
6. Place a gherkin fan on one side, and a twist of tomato on the other.

DANE'S DELIGHT

2 slices cold roast pork
buttered bread
1 tablespoon red cabbage
orange slice
lettuce
1 prune
bacon crackling (optional)

1. Place the meat on the bread in a slightly circular shape if possible.
2. Mound the red cabbage in the centre.
3. Garnish with an orange twist.
4. Tuck a small piece of lettuce and a stoned prune on opposite sides of the twist.
5. Add a small piece of crispy bacon crackling if available.

THE CONTINENTAL

lettuce
buttered bread
4 thin slices Danish salami
4 thin onion rings
parsley

1. Press lettuce into butter on one corner.
2. Fold salami slices loosely in half.
3. Arrange on buttered bread in a fan shape.
4. Snip gently through two of the onion rings.
5. Link them all together in a chain and place over the salami slices.
6. Garnish with parsley.

SHRIMP CRUSH

lettuce
buttered white bread
1 tablespoon mayonnaise
1oz (25gm) shrimps, fresh or frozen
1 lemon slice
parsley

1. Press a piece of lettuce into the buttered bread.
2. Spoon a thin line of mayonnaise down the middle of the lettuce to hold the topping.
3. Drain the shrimps well and pile them neatly on to the lettuce.
4. Spoon another thin line of mayonnaise along the top of shrimps.
5. Place a lemon twist at one end and garnish with parsley.
6. Alternatively, cover the buttered bread with lettuce.
7. Spoon on two piles of mayonnaise.
8. Sprinkle the shrimps thinly on the lettuce.
9. Garnish with a lemon twist and tomato quarters.

BLUE BOY

2 slices Danish blue cheese or Mycella
buttered bread
2 black grapes, halved

1. Cut the slices of cheese in half.
2. Arrange the slices in slightly overlapping layers on the buttered bread.
3. Garnish the top of the cheese with de-seeded black grapes.

MASTER MARINER

lettuce
buttered rye bread
1oz (25gm) pickled herring
3 onion rings
tomato
parsley sprig

1. Press a little lettuce into the butter on one corner of the bread.
2. Drain the herring well, and cut it into strips.
3. Carefully arrange three strips diagonally across each slice.
4. Garnish with three graduated onion rings across the top of the herring, and tuck a piece of tomato and a sprig of parsley into one corner by the lettuce.

LONG BOAT

2 hard-boiled eggs
1oz (25gm) butter
salt and pepper
1 tablespoon chopped pimento
2oz (50gm) prawns, chopped
few whole prawns to garnish
lettuce

1. Halve the hard-boiled eggs lengthwise.
2. Remove the yolks and mix with the butter.
3. Season well and add chopped pimento and the chopped prawns.
4. Spoon into egg hollows and garnish with whole prawns and serve on a bed of lettuce arranged on a long serving dish.

NORDIC DIP
(Illustrated on page 72)
Serves 4

4oz (100gm) cream cheese
½ teaspoon paprika pepper
½ stick celery, chopped
2oz (50gm) prawns, chopped
few drops Worcestershire sauce
salt and pepper
whole prawns to garnish
parsley

1. Mix the cream cheese with paprika pepper, chopped celery and chopped prawns. Add Worcestershire sauce and seasoning to taste.
2. Pile into a bowl and garnish with whole prawns and parsley. Sprinkle with paprika pepper and serve with snack crackers or potato crisps.

SANGRIA 1
Serves 8

Spain's popular drink; many people marinate fruit and spices in it for 24 hours.

1 bottle dry, full-bodied red wine
juice of 1 lemon
1 lemon, sliced
soda water to taste

1. Mix all ingredients together and serve well iced.

SANGRIA 2
Serves 8

For those who prefer a mixture of red wine and spirits, the following recipe is an excellent one, best made the day before and served very cold.

1 bottle dry red wine
1 glass Cognac
dash of Curaçao
sugar to taste
soda water to taste (optional)

1. Mix all ingredients together and leave overnight in cool place.
2. Serve well iced.

DANISH CHRISTMAS GLOGG
Serves 8

This is served in Denmark during the Christmas season.

1 bottle light red wine
1 small piece whole cinnamon
3–5 whole cloves or 2–3 teaspoons cardamon
strip of lemon peel
4oz (100gm) sugar
2oz (50gm) blanched almonds
2oz (50gm) seedless raisins

1. Heat the wine and spices and simmer for a few minutes over a low heat.
2. Cut the lemon peel into small strips.
3. Add the peel, sugar, almonds and raisins to the liquid.
4. Stir and leave over the heat for a few minutes. Serve warm. (If a stronger glogg is required, a third of the red wine can be replaced by port, and brandy can also be added.)

POLISH NEW YEAR'S EVE PUNCH
(Illustrated on page 72)
Serves 12

1lb (½ kilo) cube sugar
2 oranges
2 lemons
2 pints (approximately 1 litre) light white wine
1 pint (approximately ½ litre) white rum
orange and lemon slices to decorate

1. Rub sugar cubes on skins of oranges and lemons.
2. Combine with wine and rum, allow to dissolve, and add strained juice from the oranges and lemons according to taste.
3. Heat, cover, and serve piping hot with extra slices of oranges and lemons. (If punch is too strong, dilute with a little hot water. Red wine can be used for this punch in which case substitute dark rum for white.)

COFFEE COGNAC
Serves 4

A French way of serving coffee, using instant coffee.

1 pint (approximately ½ litre) boiling water
4 teaspoons instant coffee granules
4 measures Cognac
4 teaspoons sugar
4 tablespoons double cream

1. Make coffee by pouring boiling water over the coffee granules. Stir until dissolved.
2. Put brandy and sugar in each glass.
3. Add sufficient hot coffee to fill the glass three-quarters full. Stir until the sugar has dissolved.
4. Float double cream on surface by pouring it over the back of a spoon. Sip the coffee through the cream.

Basic recipes

FRENCH DRESSING

4 tablespoons olive oil
½ level teaspoon salt
¼ level teaspoon caster sugar
¼ level teaspoon freshly
ground pepper
2 tablespoons white wine
vinegar

1. Put oil into a basin and add salt, sugar and pepper.
2. Whisk in the vinegar drop by drop and continue beating until mixture thickens slightly.

Variations
Add a few chopped fresh herbs, a little crushed garlic or a dash of mustard etc.

ASPIC JELLY
Makes ½ pint or 250ml

½oz (12gm) gelatine
½ pint (250ml) boiling water
¼oz (6gm) caster sugar
¼ level teaspoon salt
2 tablespoons tarragon vinegar
2 tablespoons lemon juice

1. Dissolve gelatine in boiling water. Add all other ingredients.
2. Leave to cool and thicken.
3. Use as required either before or after it has set as the recipe demands.

Note
Alternatively, thicken a can of consommé with approximately 2 teaspoons gelatine. Or dilute clear meat extract or a bouillon cube with ½ pint (250ml) water and add approximately 2 teaspoons gelatine.

WHITE SAUCE
Makes ½ pint or 250ml

½oz (12gm) butter or margarine
½oz (12gm) flour
½ pint (250ml) cold milk (or
milk and stock or water mixed)
salt and pepper

1. Melt the butter or margarine in a pan over a gentle heat.
2. Stir in flour and cook without browning for 2 minutes, stirring all the time.
3. Remove pan from heat and gradually beat in the liquid. Alternatively, add all the liquid and whisk thoroughly.
4. Return to heat and bring to boil, stirring well. Simmer gently for 2–3 minutes and add seasoning. If sauce is to be kept, cover it with greaseproof paper or foil to prevent a skin forming.

THICK WHITE SAUCE
Makes ½ pint or 250ml

Make exactly as for white sauce, above, but double the quantities of butter or margarine and flour used.

CHEESE SAUCE
Makes ½ pint or 250ml

Make up ½ pint (250ml) white sauce (see this page). After sauce has come to the boil and thickened, add 2–4oz (50–100gm) grated cheese and ½ level teaspoon mustard. Stir sauce over low heat until cheese melts.

SHORTCRUST PASTRY
Makes 8oz or 200gm pastry

8oz (200gm) plain flour
1 level teaspoon salt
2oz (50gm) lard
2oz (50gm) butter or margarine
cold water to mix

1. Sift flour and salt into a bowl.
2. Cut fats into flour with a knife.
3. Rub fats into flour with fingertips until mixture resembles fine breadcrumbs.
4. Add water little by little, stirring with a knife until mixture forms large lumps.
5. Bring mixture together with fingertips and knead lightly into a ball.
6. Roll out briskly on a floured board. Avoid stretching the pastry.

Note
Baking temperature: moderately hot, 400 deg F or gas 6 (200 deg C).

RICH SHORTCRUST PASTRY

Make as for shortcrust pastry, above, but sift the flour with ½oz (12gm) icing sugar and mix in 1 egg before adding the water.

Note
Baking temperature: moderate to moderately hot, 375 deg F or gas 5 (190 deg C).

CHEESE PASTRY
Makes 8oz or 200gm pastry

Use for savoury pies, canapé bases, cheese straws and savoury flans.

8oz (200gm) self-raising flour
1 level teaspoon salt
pinch of cayenne pepper
2oz (50gm) lard
2oz (50gm) butter or margarine
5oz (125gm) cheese, grated
1–2 egg yolks
cold water to mix

1. Sift flour, salt and pepper into a bowl.
2. Cut fats into flour with a knife.
3. Rub fats into flour with fingertips until mixture resembles fine breadcrumbs. Add cheese.
4. Mix in egg, then add water little by little, stirring with a knife until mixture forms large lumps.
5. Bring mixture together with fingertips and knead lightly into a ball.
6. Roll out briskly on a floured board. Avoid stretching the pastry.

Note
Baking temperature: moderate, 350 deg F or gas 4 (180 deg C).

SUET CRUST PASTRY
Makes 8oz or 200gm pastry

Use for steak and kidney puddings, sweet puddings and roly polies.

8oz (200gm) self-raising flour or
8oz (200gm) plain flour plus 2
teaspoons baking powder
1 level teaspoon salt
4oz (100gm) beef or mutton
suet, shredded or grated
¼ pint (125ml) cold water

1. Sift self-raising flour (or plain flour and baking powder) into a bowl with salt.
2. Add suet then mix in water with a knife until lumps begin to form.
3. Gather mixture lightly together and knead until smooth.
4. Turn out on a floured board and shape into a ball. Leave to stand 10 minutes before using.

Note
Baking temperature: moderately hot, 400 deg F or gas 6 (200 deg C). Alternatively, steam.

FLAKY PASTRY
Makes 8oz or 200gm pastry

Use for pies, vanilla slices, sausage rolls.

8oz (200gm) plain flour
1 level teaspoon salt
3oz (75gm) lard
3oz (75gm) butter or margarine
1 teaspoon lemon juice
water to mix

1. Sift flour and salt into a bowl. Blend the fats on a plate and mark into four portions.
2. Rub one portion into the flour until it resembles fine breadcrumbs.
3. Mix to a smooth dough with lemon juice and water.
4. Knead dough lightly and roll it out on a floured surface into an oblong.
5. Dot two-thirds of the pastry with second portion of fat.
6. Fold the bottom third up and the top third over into an envelope shape.
7. Allow pastry to relax for 10 minutes in a cold place. This is especially important in warm weather.
8. Repeat the whole process until all the fat is used up.
9. Fold pastry in two, roll out to ¼–½ inch thick and use as required.

Note
Baking temperature: hot, 425 deg F or gas 7 (220 deg C).

Note
When using metric measures for
your pastry it will be necessary
to increase the amount of flour
to 225gm and other ingredients
proportionately, as 1oz is equal
to 28·35gm.

PUFF PASTRY
Makes 8oz or 200gm pastry

Use for vol au vents, bouchée cases, patties, mille feuilles, palmiers. It is essential to keep everything including hands very cold for this pastry.

8oz (200gm) plain flour
½ level teaspoon salt
8oz (200gm) unsalted butter in a block or 4oz (100gm) cooking fat and 4oz (100gm) margarine mashed and formed into a block
2 teaspoons lemon juice
6–8 tablespoons very cold water

1. Sift flour and salt into a bowl.
2. Chill the fat if soft. Rub ½oz (12gm) fat into flour.
3. Mix to a dough with lemon juice and water.
4. Roll out dough to twice the length of the block of fat. Place fat on dough and fold dough down over it, sealing edges well with a rolling pin.
5. Give pastry one half turn and roll gently out into a long strip.
6. Fold dough in three, envelope style, and leave, covered, in a cold place for 30 minutes.
7. Repeat turning, rolling and folding six times.
8. Leave pastry to relax for 30 minutes between rollings and before use.

Note
Baking temperature: hot, 450 deg F or gas 8 (230 deg C).

PANCAKE BATTER
Makes ½ pint or 250ml

4oz (100gm) plain flour
pinch of salt
1 egg
½ pint (250ml) cold milk
1 tablespoon oil

1. Sift flour and salt into a bowl.
2. Make a well in the centre and break egg into it.
3. Gradually beat in half the milk and continue beating until batter is smooth.
4. Fold in rest of milk with oil.

Index